ANOTHER SOMERSET CENTURY

*How Somerset County Cricket Club possibly became
one of the top four domestic teams in the world and
the agonies involved on the journey*

Spes est id Qvod Offendit – It is hope that hurts

CHARLES WOOD
Illustrated by the author

HALSGROVE

In memory of
Brian Langford
1935 - 2013

First published in Great Britain in 2013

Other cricket books by Charles Wood:
Bats, Pads and Cider – A Miscellany of Somerset Cricket
Bats, Pads and Gladiators – A Miscellany of Gloucestershire Cricket

Publisher's Disclaimer
As is well known, Halsgrove have disowned Mr Wood on many occasions
in the past and this particular volume is no exception. The views expressed herein arise
entirely from the fevered brain of Mr Wood who remains
entirely responsible for them, the Publisher is pleased to say.

British Library Cataloguing-in-Publication Data
A CIP record for this title is available from the British Library

ISBN 978 0 85704 214 9

HALSGROVE
Halsgrove House,
Ryelands Business Park,
Bagley Road, Wellington, Somerset TA21 9PZ
Tel: 01823 653777   Fax: 01823 216796
email: sales@halsgrove.com

Part of the Halsgrove group of companies
Information on all Halsgrove titles is available at: www.halsgrove.com

Printed and bound in China by Everbest Printing Co Ltd

The Naming of Parts

Acknowledgements

My next-door neighbour had looked at me as if I were a tad mazed. 'You've written a book about Somerset cricket with no mention of the Glory Years or of Botham, Richards and Garner? Really?'

'Pretty much,' I said. 'That's become old hat. Last century stuff. One has to move on.'

To allow me to have done so humungous thanks must go to Keith Parsons, Steffan Jones and Andy Hurry. Thanks also to Brian Rose, Vic Marks, Mervyn Kitchen, Andrew Caddick, and Mark Lathwell whose chats in odd places had put me on track. To cricket statisticians Andrew Roberts and Rajesh Kumar I extend my sincere thanks for their kind and motivational words. And a mention, too, for the inspirational pair of blackbirds nesting above my warped, blue front door.

I'm also indebted to carpenter Phillius, Mooseman, Ajit, Roy of the *Three Ferrets*, and of course to my loving wife Ali who has held me steadfast to the writing of this book through her endless encouragement.

I additionally thank Julian Davidson and Steven Pugsley at Halsgrove for their patience and regret the need for their frequent nudges over past months.

But most importantly of all, I thank Somerset County Cricket Club and the cricket lovers of the Summer Land who make the long days of warm sunshine so special for match day scribblings in a 'Moleskine' amidst the grinding tyranny of the fixture list.

Whether you play cricket in the County, write about it, think about it, live it or merely watch the odd highlights programme when there was nothing else on, you can never exhaust the unfathomable talent and quirkiness that continues to be Somerset. The cricket is too rich, too human and complex for that.

Wiveliscombe,
May 2013

PREFACE

Hope Renews

'It's no good crying over spilt milk; all we can do is bail up another cow.'
Joseph Chiefley

In the age where scorers use laptops West Country cricket can be excitingly gut wrenching in the hunt for silverware. That said, how Somerset County Cricket Club possibly became one of the top four domestic teams in the world and the agonies involved in the journey is a story worth telling.

So let's cut to the chase, this book is not fodder for the faint-hearted supporter. Here nightmares are revisited, so too the odd scandal. But it's not all tears, doldrums and tabloids. Far from it. Never has *The Blackbird* been sung more lustily, or, indeed, emotionally.

Resplendent in either cream or in scientifically designed pyjamas the County's cricket pros led by Captain 'Banger' Trescothick call themselves 'Somerset', and hope springs eternal for the summer game's popular bridesmaids now entering the 'Nosworthy era'.

For those that follow a Wyvern rag fluttering on a pole, this is the topsy-turvy, roller-coaster journey of Somerset Cricket Club passing into a new millennium and on into a decade and more of Championship jousts and the brave new world of one-day fingernail nibbling.

Scrumpy hangovers were tender whether from a bountiful year for Cox's Pippins or the second division nadir of the 'Burns Unit', and certainly from success under the gurt Biff mountain from Johannesburg to that provided by the little Langer bloke with the boxing kangaroo tattooed on his buttock. Now in the stressful era

of Banger's boys the County Championship is a chimera annually quested, players' passports hold visas, and Somerset willow has nurdled and smoked leather from Taunton to Hyderabad.

In Taunton Deane we geared up hopeful for another blooming season of it.

Flexing her considerable muscles, the handle-pulling barmaid made cider pints on tap gush and gargle into eagerly awaited glasses. Upon bar stools and around the tables of the snug *'Bearin' Up'* – the *Bear Inn* to the comfortable – men and women have turned from nursing their chilblains and shredding Valentine's Day Cards to twiddling their fingers on imagined cricket balls.

And there's no better place than the pub to twiddle because Wiveliscombe is a rarity – a cricket club without a clubhouse. We muddle through, instead, in the bowels of our singularly arcane small rugby stand. Now, with the massing of the snowdrops, shrinking violets are beginning to think of putting away the rugby posts, and sluicing down the muddied and bloodied rugby changing rooms in preparation for the lilywhite chaps.

Already beyond the rickety gate, down cidrous lanes from Dulverton in the west to Temple Cloud in the east, heavy rollers are already squashing flat the rich tilth of Somerset molehills. While in Norton St Phillip the church clock is probably checked to be in good working order. According to local folklore a wicket falls when the bells chime three. Such matters have seldom failed to keep players and spectators hanging in suspense, although I fear this to be an unfortunate term of phrase. The village team affectionately known as the 'Pitchforkers' have as their cricket ground a field where the notorious Judge Jeffreys conducted executions during the Bloody Assizes in 1685. In respect to this perhaps an umpire might be persuaded to don a black cap prior to raising a digit.

At this juncture it's probably best to start the lesser suffering of pondering where the key for Wiveliscombe's cricket 'store cupboard' was actually last put. It's an important issue for inside the squinch of spiders, rats, mice and the brittle carcasses of bluebottles lies the old school easel, the time-worn, nail studded scoreboard, and the craftsman made plates of tin numbers that along with sets of stumps and a motley array of club kit will, as sure as eggs are eggs, be dragged out into Spring daylight and seasonal hope renewed. Someone, somewhere, will inevitably start the strain of 'Somerset la-la-la, Somerset la-la-la', inviting voices from offices, shops, white vans, tractor cabs, milking parlours, up ladders and under duvets to take up the refrain.

Until then, there are the memories, many happy, several of pain.

ONE

Getting in the Flow

'This is where they live: Not here and now, but once where all happened once.'
Phillip Larkin, *The Old Fools.*

East of Frome leaves were falling in the fiefdom of 'Lord Gower', ducks quacked and every slow passing Guildford willow was a reminder of the batting rabbit in me. Rowed down the River Wey by my student son I knew full well Charles Lutwidge Dodgson aka Lewis Carroll was buried atop the nearby hill, yet felt it was I who was in Wonderland.

I asked my offspring to slow his stroke when Surrey's not very big Woodbridge Road cricket ground came into view on the left bank, and for brief moments immersed myself in reverie. Here in 2006 on a Clutterbuck pitch – prepared by groundsman of the year Bill Clutterbuck – Sir Vivian Richards had lost his record Somerset score to Alfie, that's to say Justin Langer, who had chosen a six-week sojourn instead of the alternative of facing Perth bowling machines and the 'Fremantle Doctor'. Against Surrey, the Aussie panjandrum in his one and only first-class appearance that season made 342 off 416 balls with two sixes and 43 fours in a little more than ten hours at the crease. 'Viv Richards probably got his in about three hours – that's the difference,' said Alfie modestly at the time of his achieving the 10th highest score in all first-class cricket in England. 'My greatest challenge is to master concentration – that's what I was thrilled about here,' he remarked while thanking Somerset for giving him the chance of some match practice ahead of the Ashes series that coming winter.

Splashed liberally by an oar 'catching a crab' I was returned tutting to the present where September had brought several days worthy of note. For instance, in the

hope of practice bearing fruit, Somerset's old Harrovian and leading willow maestro Nick 'Compo Dog' Compton, scratching around on the road to recovery after a bad back, had put aside his Wyvern badged helmet and batted for the white rose of Yorkshire at Taunton Vale. To get back into 'Nick', he claimed. And this having narrowly missed out on becoming the first player since 1988 to score 1,000 first-class runs before the end of May. However, as an unsuitable Tyke he did eventually see sense, and thinking 39 runs to be enough to have got his eye in again, strategically retired to allow Somerset victory by an innings in a three day friendly.

By wood of oar rather than wood of bat autumn's fruitfulness had been thrust upon me, too. A lack of offspring coordination had skulled me backwards into the blackberry plumps that prickle-draped the riverbank. A conspicuous purple stain now adorned the backside of my chinos as amid September's shortening days the 2012 County Championship trundled into being ones worthy of West Country nostalgia.

At Hove, in a match billed as Murray Goodwin's fairytale farewell with Sussex piling on the runs, things didn't quite turn out as the martlet badged ones had hoped. Somerset – Zum to some – completed the second highest run chase in their history, pulling off a five-wicket win after lunch on the fourth day.

What a turn around it had been! Shot out for just 134 on day two, then with Sussex 317 ahead with eight wickets in hand, the south-coasters were culpable of failing to profit and ultimately paid the price. With a depleted batting line-up, all Somerset's established batsmen had to stand up and Hildreth and Trego duly did. Indeed, only Compo Dog scored more first class runs over the departed summer. With Bears already on the podium, runners-up in the Championship had been up for Zum's grabs as next up Taunton beckoned the poor-travelling Pears.

Bedded down at County Ground pitch level for the match duration Zum's 'Tweet-Lord' Somerset La La La had messaged his personal view: 'Wonderful. Just wonderful. This is the very best place in the whole world.' A perception seconded by Dave's SCCC News.

At altitude, those braving the wind bashed 'Potting Shed' commentary box atop the old pavilion needed further convincing. Laconic banter by Dave Bradley guesting from BBC Hereford and Worcester had drifted away from Weed and the Flowerpot Men, Bill and Ben. With Zum ascendant Dave, a tad hot under the collar, became whingy having put his jacket on for the 50th time in a few hours: 'Like a junkyard on the roof outside here. Litter everywhere. Needs a tidy-up close season. Next time I come here I'll bring the Squeegee mops to clean the windows. Nothing but grime and spiders webs.' On the other side of the door Mrs Bradley had braced herself against gusts arriving from the Quantocks. 'Don't open the door yet,' shouted Dave, 'it's wrapped around my belt.'

Zum for their part had wrapped matters up on the third day thanks to a ton from Marcus Trescothick, Compo Dog digging in to finish unbeaten on 155, just six shy of 1,500 first-class runs for the season, and Abdur 'Manny' Rehman, a great ambassador for Pakistan cricket, tweaking away match figures of 14 for 101. A feat that deserved the match ball being mounted, engraved and presented to him.

In truth the game was largely done and dusted in its infancy when Manny produced the best bowling performance of his career. In claiming nine first innings Worcestershire wickets, he became only the tenth Zum player to ever accomplish such cheer. The last time was back in 1993, when 'Caddy Shack' Caddick claimed a career best nine for 32 to bowl out a side Lancashire, chasing 97 to win, for 72 – a match in which, out of interest, Marcus T. made his debut, stepping up to the crease as a 17-year old.

Whilst all this was going on that lover of classical music Bob 'Dylan' Willis had wittered sage-like for Sky Sports in its meaningful coverage of Zum old boys Wes Durston's and Mark Turner's Derbyshire versus Hampshire at the climax of the County Championship Division 2. Cutting away from a procession of hogs, Dylan reported on affairs in the West Country.

Gloucestershire had grabbed its eighth wooden spoon after a tight finish with Leicestershire. The scoreboard now reads Gloucester 8 Somerset 12 on that little matter. On the up side, Somerset's haul of bonus points had leapfrogged them to nestle behind the champion table-topping Bears.

'Somerset have a habit of coming second' was the throwaway line tripping off the lugubrious tongue. Absolutely Dylan, I thought, Zum might appear forever in a fugue for bridesmaids. I did a finger count. Eight times the county has been runners-up in various competitions since the start of the 2009 season. And celestial harpists could pluck their assembled strings in counting to 137 – the number years now of Zum never having won the Championship.

As ever, autumn's chill had bought up and down movement. The White Rose County scrambled up as the former champion lanky-lanky red roses slid down. And, after eight years, another Rose departed. Brian the Rose of Zum stepped down as Director of Cricket to become a blooming presence in Wales. 'I see too many people have bitter regrets because they stay on too long,' he told BBC Somerset. 'I've reached the mental stage where I knew the time was right. As a club and an individual you have to think: "where is this club going?"'

Then I'd discovered Compo Dog standing alone, mobile to his ear, near the infamous *Gordon's Wine Bar*, a fashionable dive resembling a discarded set from *Pirates of the Caribbean* tucked away on London Embankment. He was a month away from his departure, his barkless willows in bag, India bound as the new England opener. 'Hi Bru. What are you doing here?' I enquired.

After scrutinizing me as if I were an indifferent pie chucker, he volunteered, 'Not a lot going on in Taunton'.

Absolutely right, nothing at all apart from spiders web weaving undisturbed, Somerset La La La and Dave's SCCC News snoozing away in hibernation, and whispers of Manny, mad as a hatter, making himself as high as Alice while puffing away on the wacky-baccy. As Spike Milligan once chuckled: 'Everybody's got to be somewhere.'

* * *

Rain plothered down covering the windows of the 'Caddy Shack' pavilion with a coat as thick and opaque as glycerine. The rain, which had been coming and going, spattered in big gobs upon the glistening covers. The funereal black sightscreens draped in the Sir Ian Botham Stand twitched and flapped spasmodically in the wind.

Seasonal change had made the summer land of Zum a misnomer. Cricket snoozed. Daylight hours were shortening and, with a major darts event at the County Ground in its final planning stage, tungsten would soon offer the paying spectator an alternative to willow and leather, though, with an open bar, not necessarily a drier one.

Other than running droplets there was little activity apart from head groundsman Simon Lee. Between the heavy showers he would be out in the middle, a man outstanding in his field, wheelbarrow heavy with Mendip loam to hand, absorbed in autumn renovations of spiking, scarifying, top dressing, and spraying. And, of course, he'd be scratching his head as to what to do with Taunton's infamous rutted outfield, the cause of many an inconvenient and embarrassing bobble.

Overcome by a niggling impulse and about to embark on a small sojourn to the Antipodes I had emailed my long suffering publisher: 'Having deciphered more scribbles in my Moleskine diaries my waters tell me it's time to write again. Something along the lines of the continuing sagas of West County cricket – Zum, Glawster, Deb'n – with the odd mongoose, kookaburra and travelling cricketer chucked in the kitbag.'

The reply was alarmingly brief. 'Perhaps a reflection on the recent past – Zum in the Twenty First Century – never has so much been missed by so little so many times etc etc? Think of a title and get on with it.'

Blimey.

What if I called it 'Blame the Tablets on the Bridesmaids'?

Westerly gusts buffeting Pitsford Hill whirled the little cast iron batsman weathervane on the flat roof above like the thoughts in my brain.

Inside, the atmosphere was snug and full of natter. Deprived of stumps, bowlers aimed at the skittles that had taken the place of summer's tea laden tables. And Roy Tackle, acclaimed as probably the finest living groundsman in Somerset was cheerfully pulling the pints and pushing the measures in his beloved portacabin cricket pavilion-cum-pub known locally as the *Three Ferrets*.

Undoubtedly, Brompton Ralph Cricket Club had come a long way, and winds of change were blowing for the better in the grass roots.

Fifty grand's worth of Olympic legacy funding from Sport England had been allocated to renovate and to extend the changing rooms upwards to a dizzying two-storey height. This was a far cry from the recycled, twenty-foot by ten, defunct, deep litter chicken house tarted-up with a coat of white paint that had bought civilization to a field of buttercups and celandines sweated over by Roy with purpose, and a finger mower, more than a half century ago.

Putting things in context, that was when Mervyn Kitchen, Bill Alley and Ken Palmer were making up the County's middle order under Colin Atkinson's watchful skipper's eye.

So drawing on hindsight, Roy was living proof that everyone benefits from a place to belong – a lesson which oddly at County level didn't stick in the head straight away.

Unlike Roy, who comfortably mixed business with cricketing pleasure, Zum has had a truculent evolution since the County club was formed haphazardly, beyond border patrols of weasels, in Devon, in 1875, with a resolution declaring: 'There shall be no county ground.' Of course, that was a whimsy as daft as a bag of frogs. A few marshy acres in Taunton soon put that right, although the subsequent naming of parts continues to raise eyebrows.

Take, Bicknoller's Harold Gimblett. To many retiring minds he remains Zum's greatest homegrown batsmen. Harold has the little hill in front of St James's church named in his honour that could have been the afternoon's work for a few letharic moles. The 'Caddy Shack', the newest of the current triad of pavilions, muted as a triage of age, acknowledges the length and line of Andrew Caddick. A grand set of gates honour Sir Vivian Richards whilst Joel Garner has little more than a turnstile. And whereas a gurt stand is dedicated to Sir Ian 'Beefy' Botham, present skip, Marcus Trescothick has his moniker on a piddly one.

Now rumours were abroad about the draughty rooftop potting shed of a commentary box being endangered along with the historic Old Pavilion. Gossip

circulated that they were to be replaced by a purpose built media centre, corporate facilities and seating for the affluent. Already one or two artistic types were hard at it designing placards of pithy protest.

But who knew what grand design might emerge from an architect's cupboard should Keynsham's finest son Marcus finally lead Zum to win their first ever County Championship – or anything else for that matter – following a series of blips. 2012 had been the first year in four Somerset hadn't made the final of the t20. Chris Gayle was supposed to help them actually win the tournament. It was there in black and white. Yet, the year's *Playfair Cricket Annual* had jumped the gun including his resume amongst the Somerset squad members. Instead, the giant tonker from Excelsior turned up unexpectedly in a West Indies changing room without batting an eyelid. Zum's next choice Roelof van der Merwe then failed to secure a visa for reasons best known to the Home Office.

Unsurprising then that the Wyvern rag had been at half mast at the Swalec after a semi-final batting non event against Hampshire when nobody save Craig 'Hobnob' Kieswetter had got out of second gear.

His long legs straddling a small table, his cider glass half empty my stump thin factotum carpenter and boat builder friend Phillius slouched and whinged. 'Trego's tattoos will be wrinkly and Compo Dog will be gainfully employed in some God awful remake of *Last of the Summer Wine* before Zum struggles choking over the line. And by that time even Glawster will have won the sodding County Championship.'

Sharing the table with Phillius and myself, liberal-minded Becky delaying a sip of her Bloody Mary tried to remain positive. 'Oh c'mon, there's nothing wrong in coming second,' she said.

'You don't understand, luv.'

'Oh don't I? Last time I looked there were eighteen teams. Twenty-one if you include the Scots, Dutch and the … Unicorns.'

'We're not talking about one-dayers now. Heck, we know about them. Saying that, when it comes down to the nitty-gritty, what matters most is the cut and thrust of the West Country. Zum and Glawster. Scrumpy barrel versus scrumpy barrel.'

'And what about Worcester?'

'What about Worcester? They're mere middling pear crunchers.'

Bless the intoxicating subjects of fruit juice and cricket. Trying to keep a straight

face, I butted in. 'Manchester's got itself a thriving community scrumping initiative in Moss Side. Lancashire cider's now ready to sell to the world. Might that qualify Red Roses as scrumpy quaffers, too?'

'No!' said Phillius and Anita, for once in mutual agreement.

'Anyway,' I said, 'name the last meaningful battle between Zum and Glawster?

'1999!' was the chorus erupting from the neighbouring eavesdroppers. Pity was, to those in Zum, the bragging rights to silverware had remained north of Frome well into the new millennium. And this despite the vaulted 'Banger' led firepower that had recently spluttered due to the weather. Without doubt the West Country undeniably had had a sinking feeling.

Glawster having sunk to the very bottom of the County Championship were being called 'Denizens of the Deep'. News was that Captain 'Giddo' had drowned in sorrow and a Klinger was asked to skipper wreckage whose batting tail had less wag than a despondent gun dog.

Happily, Captain Trescothick navigated a more buoyant course. After silent prayers were said over his dodgy ankle he had signed a new three-year contract with an optimistic flourish just as Somerset became a waterworld.

Admittedly, towards the latter end of an Olympic year it wasn't quite the Tsunami of 1607 that put an end to games of stob-ball.

Nor was it quite as bad as the great flood of 1929 when swallows flew low forecasting rain before the new moon stood on end and emptied the rivers out at the time Holford's 'Farmer' White led both Somerset and England whilst Gloucestershire's bespectacled kingpin B.H. Lyon became outspoken on cricket captaincy and tradition.

But that said, it was ruddy miserable outside. Cider apple trees, heavy with mistletoe, stood stoic in Zum's waterslain Levels. The withy beds had gone under. And with regard to cricket the grass roots were submerged.

A bedraggled Steve Nelson of Taunton Deane Cricket Club told journos: 'we were flooded a few months ago but this is much worse, another six inches higher and rising.' Of course the boys and girls of the local press lapped it up.

As cricketing contests went, Duckworth Lewis had become an everyday computation back in our soggy summer of happy mallards having got wetter and wetter.

And there were more than enough ducks to be had in a window of opportunity just before mid summer to put Somerset cricket on the homepage of BBC news.

The article itself was small yet its content prompted a toast to be raised in gratitude in Wiveliscombe. Which meant for once it wasn't a report from the County Ground or from anywhere else on the professional circuit causing Summerlanders to fall down in a faint.

Instead, the story centred on the larks of Barrington. Its village cricket eleven had trumped the local news of three rooms at Barrington Court being filled with Antony Gormley's acclaimed work, *Field for the British Isles*, consisting of 40,000 small clay figures.

However, it wasn't fielding that was the concern of Barrington as the summer game came under the microscope. It was a batting embarrassment that Gormley's packed crowd couldn't witness.

Playing away at Huish & Langport beside the muddied banks of the Parrett in Division 2 of the Shrubbery Barrington had by misfortune bagged a West Country record that had stood for over one and a half centuries.

Mooseman, a Somerset cricket lover of artistic persuasion, felt the need to comment on one of the lowest scores ever in a senior match. 'Well, pick any eleven from Gormley's throng of thousands and I'm sure none could have done any worse.'

That, to be fair, was a slight exaggeration. The fateful innings had started swimmingly. Barrington managed to put their first three runs on the board without losing a wicket. Openers Tim Towill and Steve Redwood, though not exactly household names common to the daily sports pages, had at least both got starts – 2 and 1 respectively. Further down the order at number 7 Mark Jennings also nicked a single. The problem lay in the remaining eight batters getting quackers. Only the generosity of a couple of extras rounded things up to an all out score of a full half dozen. At last, at long, long last Wiveliscombe lost the smirch its cricket team had held since 1857 when they managed a measly 8.

I recalled how few balls were larruped across the West Country as July emerged from June to hail in the London Olympics, and cricketers continually huddled in damp pavilions. One in particular became excessively so.

Devon's swollen River Otter had broken its banks and drowned more than the local cow parsley. Budleigh Salterton Cricket Club truly earned its nickname 'The Otters'. Their cricket pitch was somewhere, several feet under, invisible to the naked eye. However, there were hints. A wet-suited kitesurfing youth had been whooping and a-yelling using the sloping roof of Budleigh's still submerged wooden pavilion as a take off ramp for 'big air' and 'kiteloops'.

Inside, in the pavilion's bar, beneath the flood and clinked by torrent-borne beer

and cider glasses, a 'Health and Safety' fire extinguisher sticker seemed pecu-
liarly ironic. Thankfully, cricket bats holding memories of worthy innings
managed to cling on to their high mounted racks.

Like a plea for help, the sign nailed to the outside wall read 'Visitors Welcome'.
With bare knees, sandals, a red life vest, and sunglasses perched on his nose, Mr
White, no relation to 'Farmer', paddled passed in his yellow canoe.

Away in the foothills of the Quantocks Phillus, with local orders for three small
wooden craft, had, instead contemplated, an ark. We mused that Great Britain
still holds the Olympic title for cricket won in 1900 against France by bods from
the Devon and Somerset Wanderers in the Velodrome de Vincennes. 'We should
create Aquacket,' Phillius suggested. 'It would be a cross between swimming and
cricket.'

'Sounds more like a name for a duck,' I said.

Yes, but given the weather surely we could've won gold.'

'Not us, the Otters,' I corrected.

'You do realize he represents creativity in the West Country?' said Gill, sitting
down straight in a trained example of Alexander technique.

'What? Phillius?' I asked.

'No, the Willow Man. My hubby and I were just discussing it.' Gill's gurt husband
Jeremy croaked something inaudible, his deep bass still in recovery from
endlessly 'taking it from the top' while on choral duty for *The Hobbit* soundtrack.

Opinion was divided on the recent renovation undergone beside the M5 grockle
run before the sog set in. The largest willow figure in our Sceptred Isle, and quite
possibly the world, had had a makeover.

'Well, that bundle of withies is no Jos Buttler,' I said.

Phillius' eyes twinkled. 'I agree. Total nonsense not to have given him a cricket
bat.' A swisher and swoosher outside off stump, Phillius had a love of water akin
to that of a water rat; though *Wind in the Willows* had a totally different connota-
tion to him than it did to Kenneth Grahame.

'He's more bowlerish,' I offered, 'bit like Pete Trego or the Great Alfonso celebrating a wicket.'

'Well, had Serena de la Hey weaved a set of stumps in front of the bloody thing

he'd look more like Jamie or Craig signalling a wide,' butted in the eccentrically wired Mooseman listening in. His interjection was a harp back to the Devonian Overton twins umpiring an under-9s game at Westward Ho! 24-hours after they left the field upon Zum getting a draw in the County Championship match at the Kia Oval earlier in the year.

'You cricket dafties,' said Gill, 'he's got his arms out to stop Morrisons getting any closer.'

'I think you'll find that's what the moat's for,' offered Phillius before giving her a condescending grin.

Jeremy emerged from what seemed like deep sleep to look me in the eye.
'With Serena being South African, the probability is that it would be Alfonso Thomas.'

'But if it's the pride of Bridgwater that could make it Richard Harden, or more likely Steffan Jones,' said Phillius.

Perched on my barstool listening to arguments, the real question was: where was the best place in the world? It had to be sat on a bench on Gimblett Hill, I thought. Failing that, perched on a wall in dimpsey light on a clear evening where a wooded hill tumbles down to muddy Porlock Weir and the Bristol Channel, eating fish and chips prepared in the tiny *Exmoor Cooking Company* shed. Perhaps, the local handlebar moustached musician would play his harmonica and guitar while murdering *In the Country* by the harbour rail. It wasn't cricket, but after season's end it was sure as dammit the next best thing. Wonderland, indeed.

TWO

Millennium Bridge

'In every sport there comes a time when one era ends and another
begins. One generation must give way to the next. But it is critical
that the baton is handed over by the old to the new.'

Vasant Raiji, *Cricket Memoirs.*

In those drab years between Botham's pomp and the millennium, perhaps rather than swinging with the gusto of a rusty gate in a south westerly gale, disciplined batting was what had been needed in the summer land of Zum – Somerset to the uninitiated – where a wind of change had turned willow leaves into trembling hints of silver.

In truth there had been more than just a hint.

So much so that Phillius had become prone to philosophy at the close of the each cricket season, wallowing in the mood of a scrumpy addled Confucius. 'At summer's end a chap falls off an Somerset cliff, saves himself by clutching at a blackberry bush, and then notices a team of mice are gnawing away the branch on which his heart and soul depends. There's a fat blackberry growing on the branch, which the chap plucks and eats. The fruit tastes wonderful. The moral is,' he sighed, 'It'll come to the same thing in the end. So enjoy while you can.' Pessimistic old bugger yet as things seem to turn out he spoke very, very true.

We were three men in a newly launched skiff bobbing about in the Bristol Channel, waiting for the tide to turn, rod dangling for codling and hobbit sharks with a bait box slimy full of stinky squid more slippery to grasp than a thick outside edge. It all made for a grand way for Phillius, Bruce and me to pass the

afternoon of 21 October 2012 having no cricket to watch.

Phillius had lovingly conceived the *Maggie Jane* up in an isolated barn loft with views of the Quantock foothills. Built over ancient bat-poo-bejeweled floorboards she had been sawn, pegged, glued, planed, sandpapered and painted, with Phillius all the while turning half an ear to Test Match Special and internet commentaries of matches involving Somerset.

Capable of a devilish leg-break, Bruce was known to take Watchet harbour's seaworthy old motor torpedo boat *HMS Gay Archer* out to generate a few ripples. He liked to think the name was in memory of one the Victorian bowmen that had once fired competitive shafts between cricket games around the time Taunton Athletic Society's marshy Rack Field evolved into the County Ground.

However, the boat that had once escorted a Royal family to the Houses of Parliament was left moored, or more accurately, forlornly mud-stuck, below the Ancient Mariner statue. Bruce had accepted the invite to spend sociable time aboard Phillius' more intimate craft.

Well over the honeymoon stage with his cigarettes – nicotine marching through his veins – Bruce got the fidgets, repeatedly feeling the pocket of his flotation jacket. Obviously he was hiding something. For a few hours he restrained the urge, but in the end he just couldn't help himself. He fired his potato gun. 'Hip hip hooray for Trafalgar Day!' he shouted, before grinning like an idiot. 'Hip hip Hooray, echoed both Phillius and I. And we raised our hip flasks in a toast of apple brandy.

As an excuse for another swig, I offered: 'Here's to the bridesmaids.'

"The bridesmaids!' came the dual response.

'And for their glories to come!' roared Phillius, knocking back the dregs. Oh, bless him for being bloody positive for once, I thought. I'd tried to be for the past thirty odd years, ever since the 'Glory Years' disappeared, lost in the fogs of scrumpy, not to mention cider brandy.

And to be fair, even the 'Glory Years' had their episode of ignominy, and I'm not even going to mention the Battle of Shepton Mallet spurred on by the arrival of the polished Kiwi Crowe.

Music stirs the memory. And so it was when the Smashing Pumpkins' *1979* suddenly became audible, a tinny sound emitted from my briny braving iPod. The little number may once have gained a nomination for Record of the Year at the Grammy Awards, but it also focused the mind.

His playing days over and five trophies under his belt, that man of Kent, Harry the Teacher aka Captain Marvel, Brian, The Rose of Zum and England, could wear a lumberjack shirt and walk his pooch across Burnham pastures. In his car boot niblicks and putters had long replaced the trusted bat that had tamed the fearsome Windies attack of 1980.

Maybe, we can shuffle under the carpet Harry's infamous, nay shortsighted, decision. However, to declare that Zum innings closed against Worcestershire in a Benson and Hedges Cup zonal match after one over was grotty in the extreme. Yes, it was done to ensure Zum progressed through the group on run-rate, but as a public relations exercise it raised hackles. Gareth, a longtime supporter of Glamorgan and a master of understatement, still speaks of wanting audacious Harry 'consumed by the dragons in Ivor the Engine's firebox'. He has a point. At New Road in May '79 most spectators hadn't even taken their seats by the time the game was over.

One man who'd driven 150 miles to watch the game angrily told the thin scattering of journos he'd decided to become a Somerset member. 'But I'm damned if I will now!' he exclaimed. Another, a schoolteacher who had brought a coachload of children to see the match, spoke from his heart: 'The kind of lesson we have seen today is one no boy ought to be taught.' Spectators at Zum's next game after the fiasco had a lighter dig. 'IT'S BRIAN ROSE I DO DECLARE!' announced a homemade banner. It was only during the Windies Tour that Harry discovered that he needed to wear glasses – too late to focus on the finer points of sportsmanship.

However, rose tinted spectacles or not, let's be matter-of-fact about it, Zum captains lead by example. Take, for instance, Chris Tavaré. After being told to hop it from Kent with a sour taste in the mouth in '88, he became the studious, proper speaking stoic of Taunton for four seasons.

Taking to captaincy like a duck to water, Tav was unflappable in his demeanour and in the way he batted, building an innings with the watchfulness of any one of my marigold munching patio snails. When it came to the cricketer's art it was like watching paint dry. Or to put it another way, Tav trying to explain the nuances of death bowling in t20s is a bit like the doyen of the commentary box, Richie Benaud, discussing mobile phone apps.

Tav's Oxford blue bore no relation to the colour of a firework's touch paper. When the time came to find Tav's successor at the end of the '93 season nobody on Zum's radar seemed that interested. There had been hopes of luring John Morris from Derbyshire or James Whitaker from Leicestershire. When those plans fell apart Andy Hayhurst was internally promoted, as much, it was a said, for his calm and common sense as for the traditional reason of him being the best player in the team.

The first few matches under Hayhurst's guidance were disastrous, with the first eight competitive matches lost seemed to want to hold a hand up. So Davy-hulme's finest son of all-round talent drew the short straw. And within two years he'd been forced out in an undignified putsch. I was reminded of this when Phillius opened his generously sized lunchbox.

'Nothing like wild mushrooms to add flavor to autumn fare,' mused Phillius, upon revealing cold saddle of rabbit with ceps.

'Stuff to tickle the memories', I said enviously, but with conviction. A memory prod can happen through any sudden fusion of sound and niff. For whereas the wonders of technology like Snicko, Hot Spot and Hawkeye permit cricket commentators to express self-righteous indignation toward umpiring decisions, a Somerset fungi forager cannot ignore a buzz of flies and a wrinkled schnozzle at something akin to the offensive stench of rotting meat.

The immodest stinkhorn, or *Phallus impudicus* to give it the Latin, may cause a prude to blush and bring back the nightmare of '96 a year when Zum contrived to win something – the interest of tabloid muckrakers. Maybe as news it wasn't as high profile as Shepton Mallet but it was really most unpleasant.

Perturbing as the stinkhorn and as poisonous and damaging to the constitution as a common inkcap, scandal had caught Andy Hayhurst in its fallout, sending him packing to his semi-detached up in the Blackdown Hills. Indeed, the writer Isaac Babel was astute enough to note 'no iron can stab the heart with such force as a full stop put in the right place'.

'Poison pen sex scandal rocks county' trumpeted the *Sunday Mirror* that September after a reporter was tipped-off about anonymous letters accusing top players of having affairs having been posted to their spouses. Hell's bells, the letters contained intimate details of players private lives with the warning: 'it's happened to me. Don't let it happen to you.'

A leak from the club revealed: 'The letters were hand-written and went right to the hearts of the players' wives. If the idea was to nobble the club, then it appears to have worked.'

Although Hayhurst denied responsibility for the letters, the finger was pointed at him. The reason? He'd temporarily split from his wife April late the previous year. 'Never in all my years at the bottom and top levels of cricket have I come across anything like this,' he lamented. Neither calm nor common sense was cited in his defence.

And in an attempted cover-up of the grim episode the club blamed Hayhurst's sudden absence from the team sheet on 'a string of poor performances'.

Other players, too, suffered a noticeable drop in form. A senior player had cause to gripe: 'Andy's game undoubtedly suffered because of all this. The other players and their wives were really upset and angry.' Behind the scenes the club beavered away to find out who had been responsible, but with no luck. The speculation and mood of suspicion that surrounded the furore had an indisputably detrimental affect on team morale.

Until the season's end the discarded skipper got replaced by son of Bridgwater Richard Harden, a chap celebrating his benefit after ten years with the club. Now having the bonus fillip of captaincy he too was sought out. A *Sunday Mirror* reporter turning up at Richard's Trull farmhouse was told by Nicki, his pregnant New Zealand-born wife: 'we did receive one of the letters. It seems to be from someone very vicious. I don't know what it was all about.' And that in effect summed things up pretty well.

Only when emotions had died down did Zum look to appoint a new full-time skipper.

Fate had it that Tasmanian connections would now begin. The Club plumped for the legally-minded, Devon-born, Tazzie raised, Peter Bowler, regarded by many as one of the best players never to play Test cricket, came and opened the batting. A chum of mine with a scientific bent and an infectious chuckle named him 'Cantareus asperses'. Although, perhaps, intimating an element of horsepower and quick scoring, the name tickled his sense of humour. It, too, meant a common-a-garden snail.

To be fair Peter himself recalled a spectator heckle 'it's like listening to paint dry.' Lucky such words were aimed at such a self-effacing soul.

However, in the cash-strapped times of our age, Peter himself was aware that he had a certain usefulness. 'I was the greatest generator of income for clubs, greater than Flintoff, Botham and the rest,' he told a meeting of the Cricket Society in 2011. 'Whenever I went out to bat, the stands emptied and bars and restaurants were filled to capacity.'

Peter made way for the tough true-blooded Tasmanian Jamie Cox to kick Zum's backside out the 20th century. This he did ably assisted by Dermot Reeve who had arrived at the beginning of Peter's captaincy year.

And at the same time Andy Hayhurst, trying to get is life back, had jumped ship to coach Derbyshire's Second XI, while Colin Wells, a cricketer of booming shots and crafty medium pace, made the opposite move for a two year spell as Somerset's second XI coach and captain. It was all change at the County Ground.

Dermot had an eye for potential and work ethic and he looked to enrol.

In came a talented sixteen-year old called Peter Trego. In too, and towards the top of Dermot's list, was a rugby loving, trainee teacher Steffan Jones who on occasions wasn't averse to a spot of cricket, something he'd first shown when opening the bowling for his home village Llangennech in tandem with Simon Jones. However, it was umpires Mark Benson and Ray Julian that tipped off Dermot after having admired PGCE student Steffan cause Derbyshire batting problems in a preseason game against Cambridge University and telling him he was 'as good as any youngster out there'.

Steffan explained to me what happened next. 'I was on the teaching practice in Essex somewhere, and the headmaster came and said: "there's a phone call from Dermot Reeve". Dermott Reeve was big. He'd just finished with Warwickshire and said come down and have a trial. The Seconds were playing Kent in Ashford. So I went down.

'I bowled alright. Keith Parsons dropped a couple of catches at slip. Funny thing is, we moved him down to fine leg and he dropped one down there as well.

'When it was our turn to bat Marcus Trescothick got out shortly before the close of play. In those days he was such an annoying little toe-rag doing things like coming up behind you and flicking your ear. Small and immature stuff.' Steffan chuckled. 'I can get away with saying that as I was Marcus' Best Man at his wedding and he's Godparent to my two kids.

'Back in the changing rooms Colin Wells said: "who wants to do nightwatch-man?" I didn't even know what nightwatchman was then. I was a rugby player, loved playing sports, schoolboy international and all that. I just loved playing and expressing myself. So I said, "I'll do it. Whatever it is, I'll do it." I went in. And there was this spin bowler bowling. As far as I'm concerned spin bowlers should-n't be bowling at all. First ball, I charged down the wicket. Boom. Hit it straight back at him and he caught it. And I went, "Oh, okay."

'As I walked back Jason Kerr was in hysterics as he walked passed me as if think-ing: "what *have* you just done?" I got in the changing room a sat down and there was a row of Colin Wells and others and everyone just burst out laughing. "You've never done nightwatchman before have you?" Colin said.

"What am I supposed to do then?" I replied.

"You're supposed to block. It's to protect the one coming in."

"Oh, sorry."'

However, it wasn't a lesson learned. Two years later, first ball, nightwatchman, same place. But this time Steffan got a leading edge that was caught by Nigel

Llong. To be fair to him it was more of a defensive shot that went up. Keith Parsons muttered in passing: 'you're not doing nightwatchman here again.'

When Dermot called Steffan down he was still a rugby player. He'd played two years at Bristol and Exeter and needed to make a decision. In the end Dermot made it for him. 'Well, we'll give you a two year contract at Somerset,' he told the Welshman, going on to say he believed Steffan could make a go of it 'picking something he could be better than anyone else at'. What Somerset got was a rarity – an unstinting bowler who could bowl as quick at 6.30 in evening as he could at 11.00 in the morning.

Trescothick meanwhile got a comeuppance that perhaps changed him into the cricketer Nasser Hussain described as 'hefty, knock-kneed and genial'. Towards the end of a seven year famine passed in and out of the Somerset 1st XI he flicked the ear once too often of one hailed by Vic Marks in *Wisden* as being a member of 'a glittering triumvirate of wrist-spinners who adorn the modern game', Mushtaq Ahmed. His patience threadbare, 'Mushy' snapped one wet day at Trafford Trafford. There would be no naughty corner for Marcus. Instead the Somerset boys tied him up, carried him out to the middle of the square and without ceremony plonked him down. There, trussed like an oven ready hare, he was deserted in the rain and left to ponder on a tad more than a diet, in no particular order, of sausages, chips, sausages, toast, sausages, beans, sausages, cheese, sausages, eggs, and the occasional sausage.

Seemingly better at learning lessons than Steffan, in '99, upon a pacy Taunton pitch against Glamorgan while Duncan Fletcher was their coach, he made a stonking 167, with five sixes, when the next-best score was 50. With the touch paper finally lit he went onto to become massive in more than a gutsy sense.

So perhaps, mountains were made out of molehills as the forecasters around the Quantocks, Poldens, Mendips and Taunton Deane hummed and harred about prospects. Although, looking for portents, the Millenium Bridge was proving wobbly east of Frome. While at Alton Towers, *Hex – The Legend of the Towers* was new, too, and boasted a 'Madhouse Ride' finale. It might just as well have been a description of on-field cricketing shenanigans repeatedly played out beside the towering sandstone of boundary looming St James' church and skulking St Mary Magdalene in its shadow.

I considered all this as the tide finally turned and Phillius gunned the outboard to send the *Maggie Jane* chopping her way over the drowned mudflats back into Watchet.

THREE

Cock-Up and Dunk In

'All our best heroes are losers.'

Richard Glover, radio presenter.

Despite exuding confidence, too many years at Broken Biscuit Company – that's to say BBC – local radio appeared to have turned programme host Dominic Cotter prematurely grey. Just prior going live on air he scrutinized his studio guest across the table of microphones – an appraisal which I found unsettling. 'Thanks for coming all the way up from Somerset,' he said.

'Yep, managed to run the gauntlet around the border's weasel patrols,' I responded, adding a little less flippantly, 'I hear you don't like cricket.'

'Oh, I don't mind it. Who said I didn't?'

'Faye.'

Dominic looked indignantly through the studio class to his colleague. 'I've watched a few games at Taunton,' he muttered as a music track of something God-awful from an embarrassing era faded out to cut short any further elucidation.

Cue the cricket feature. I cast my eyes over again a helpful note handed to me by BBC Radio Gloucestershire's Faye Hatcher before going 'on air' that identified three audio highlights of Shire cricket intended for use in the morning show. A 'researcher' had trawled the denizen deeps and unearthed snippets of archived BBC commentary. They included, the note said, the 'last ball of Benson & Hedges Final 1999'.

Faye had flicked a strand of blond hair away from her eyes. 'You okay with these?'

'Absolutely.' I'd said.

Benson and Hedges Final? Easy-peasy. Glawster got the wood over the Tykes in the first domestic final played in front of 'Cherie Blair's Mouth' – the architectural award winning and very expensive Lord's media centre with its huge glass frontage at the Nursery End of the ground.

But, more fool me for being blasé. Proctor's 1977 hat-trick against Hampshire, and Jack Russell's Test hundred against India at Lords came and went, Everything was hunky-dory on all things Gloucestershire. Then came the unexpected and thank gawd these were the local airwaves largely restricted to north of Bristol, otherwise I could imagine spluttered cries of 'oh my flibbertigibbets', and the slopped morning beverages of the Zum unwarned. The excited Steve Kitchen commentary piped into my headphones wasn't the moment of white rose agony but still that a Rose nonetheless, concluding Zum's last competitive match of the '90s. 'Rose is out, caught Windows, bowled Harvey!'

After thirteen years, the tenderer souls of Somerset supporters had yet to heal.

Tweaking the knobs at her studio console Faye blushed red. Dominic Cotter failed miserably trying to appear nonplussed. I had to endure. This was the NatWest. And Graham Rose's wicket the last of Zum's to fall in the 'Cider Final'. To cap that, then came Alastair Durden describing the Shire's triumphant lifting of the wretched cup.

There'd been cock-up – something to do with labelling. But it didn't really matter having seen the shock of events for myself, allegiance torn, not quite as compelled as my Uncle Tubby to jump up and down and beat the air of Lord's with fists.

The chap who a couple of seasons years earlier was voted *All Rounder of the Year* after scoring 852 runs and taking and 63 wickets during probably his best season for the Zum, and in his benefit year, to boot, had dragged himself off the pitch distraught with disappointment as the Shire skipped and danced.

Many in the Summer Land, and indeed elsewhere, had thought Graham Rose unlucky not to receive international recognition, especially after walloping a world record 110 off 36 balls for Zum against Devon in Torquay in 1990. Somerset Chief Executive Peter Anderson, for instance, felt justified in commenting 'why he never got a One Day England cap is quite unbelievable … the selectors never looked west.' On the great occasion every cricket loving man, woman and dog had looked west it had been neither Graham's nor Zum's day.

However, Graham could count himself lucky to even play. He had taken the last

bowling slot on the team sheet as a 'thank you' for his past services rendered rather than on form. To get him in the side Somerset had had to drop Steffan Jones their leading wicket taker. Confident of his place on merit, the first Steffan got wind of things being amiss was on the eve of the match itself by inadvertently overhearing a discussion between Marcus Trescothick and Jason Kerr as they went to get some food. At the time it just caused Steffan a touch of anxiety, but little else. It only became official on the morning of the match. The news was undiplomatically broken in the nets that neither Steffan nor indeed his closest competition Matt Bulbeck had the slot. Irritatingly for both guys, Rose 'played rubbish' and the incident was proof of cricketers not talking to one another faces but, instead, gossiping behind one another's backs and consequently causing the hump.

That said, the first ever meeting between Zum and 'Glawster' in a major final had, for 29,000 bods, been a 'moving experience' given the volume of traffic heading east along the M4 corridor.

Jamie Cox, in his first year as Somerset captain, and Dermot Reeve as coach had, a short space of time, transformed sleepy Somerset into a competitive side. When Somerset went to Capetown preseason, Coxy came and joined them and became tied in adamant he was going to be a big influence on the club. Straightaway he had been true to his word.

Derm was a bit different. He had arrived from Warwickshire in '97 under a cloud – the fug of marijuana – albeit imbibed out of season while captaining the county and playing for England mid decade. However, as Abdur Rehman had recently testified such doings can have a minimal effect on the pitch. Anyway, there was more concern over Derm's guitar.

'All sportsmen, to some degree, die a death in far-off forgotten hotel rooms,' Mike Atherton had said when talking about experiences on tour with England and considered the reality of enduring 12 hours in a train carriage with Dermot Reeve and his guitar was 'enough to make anyone feel utterly dishevelled'. Thank goodness Cox gave Somerset balance.

Yet it should never be forgotten Derm was fantastic cricketer. He thought of the playing areas and little bits here and there. He weeded out slackers and tried a few different training regimes. Even before Coxy's arrival he had transformed the dressing room, made the team play smarter cricket, and ensured that the players were aware of diet and nutrition. Ultra keen, he was really the first coach Somerset had that was big on getting people fit and into athletes unlike the players from the 'Glory Years' whom he might have described as 'traditional'. No more Nigel Popplewell training in a dirty raincoat or Mervyn Kitchen's rolling gait.

Derm was seven or eight years ahead of his time and still doesn't get credit for it.

He brought in innovation like the reverse sweep and paid attention to detail. Then there were the small percentages by which he tried to improve the team. For instance if a bowler was to bowl a slow ball he had to have had a signal. Steffan Jones used to pinch the Wyvern on the shirt so Rob Turner would know what to expect. Rob would then walk up to the stumps to ensure any edge carrying. And if Rob didn't do it Dermott would get angry. He also drummed in that fielders should never be still. Instead, they should be 'on a piece of string'. So if a ball was being thrown in from somewhere in the field and a bod was stood at fine leg there's no reason for him not to be doing anything. He had to run round. It was just the sort of stuff that wasn't in the game then. And Somerset and Gloucestershire were the first one's to do it. Such basic things are the norm now but back in '99 the right teams were in the final.

And once ensconced at Lord's the crowd rose, not for a Mexican wave, but for a raucous chorus of 'Stand up if you're West Country'. Aunt Bettie became overwhelmed and a tad teary-eyed, helped along by breakfasting on a third of a bottle of Blue Sapphire gin innocently concealed in a rolled-up copy of the *Daily Telegraph*.

On that sun-drenched early autumn morning without much evidence of dew, the coin was flicked towards a few puffy white clouds overhead. 'Ah, I do believe Somerset have won the toss,' exclaimed Uncle Robert a little too smugly. 'We'll have a bat, I think'.

And then … oh Jamie, Jamie, Jamie … Cox was swayed by the tradition of Lord's finals. The side batting second had a habit of winning. Maybe egged on by advice from senior members of the Zum staff, maybe from the inexperience of some of his players, or maybe from just a feeling in his waters, JC put the Shire in.

'What a good lad,' Tubby remarked having a quiet puff of his pipe. 'Must be keen on fitness. Nothing like a bit a early morning leather chasing to get the blood pumping.' This from a fellow would rather spend time coaxing his pet African Grey Parrot, or 'Psittacine of the Shire' as he called her, to shriek 'Glawster!'

'The Tazzie wazzock!' exclaimed my Uncle Robert, Betty's other half, more to himself than to the world round about. Betty admonished him, using a liver-spotted hand to slap his knee with practiced accuracy.

'Behave,' she scolded. Robert gave her a hurtful look. 'You don't understand, my dear.'

Despite making me cringe, Robert was right to have cause for disquiet. Zum's attack had been whispered as one-dimensional and the Shire's eavesdroppers knew it. Their mantra for the day was: 'See off Caddick'. They believed that when in came to Cox's red-faced pippins there were to be easy pickings. And this

certainly wasn't based on the judgment of maidens.

Twenty-seven overs into the Shire innings and the opening duo of Kim Barnett and Tim Hancock had cracked and nurdled their way to putting 127 on the board. Robert was given cause to mutter 'they've rather taken a fancy to our medium-pacers.' His was no understatement. Jarvis and Rose had haemorrhaged runs, releasing any pre match pressure of Shire nerves.

Then came hope in the guise of Keith Parsons being a dead-eyed-dick from short mid wicket. In a flash it was Barnett who was the one short, desiring of a single for his fifty.

However, their basis well and truly laid, the Shire effectively defended a score of 230 for eight by taking the first five Somerset wickets for 52. Jack Russell succeeded in driving more than one Zum batsman to distraction by his antics behind the stumps. Here, one can only interpret the words of the Shire's coach John Bracewell when he said, ' I've always believed the wicketkeeper orchestrates what goes on in the field if he is *offensive* in his attitude.'

Indeed, earlier in the match Jack had caused Andy Caddick to lose his cool by backing up too far during a valuable cameo innings that produced an unbeaten 31 and trademark extravagant leaving of the ball outside off stump.

Zum though, through Rob Turner and Keith Parsons, added 82 for their sixth wicket. Despite that partnership the last four went down for 14, and there were almost five overs left when Ian Harvey concluded the game.

Tim Hancock's aggressive 74 was the focal point of the Shire innings, although a target of 231 should have been gettable. Surely, none in the crowd could forget the anguished cry of 'NO!' from Jamie Cox that seemed to echo around Lord's when he was trapped ell bee by Mike Smith after only having faced four balls. And Jack Russell snaffling Trescothick easy as pie off Boo Boo Alleyne put paid to the rest of Betty's gin. Banger, out for 5, had clobbered just the single boundary.

Come the end of the game, three wickets each for Harvey, Alleyne and Smith made certain of a notable double. Jack Russell had four dismissals, three catches and a memorable stumping while standing up to the medium-fast bowling of Mike Smith. By whipping off the bails in a flash as Keith Parsons fatally let his foot drag, Jack effectively ended Zum's hopes of catching the Shire's total. To popular acclaim, his contribution with bat and gloves earned him Man of the Match.

Looking back now, for a first season as captain of Somerset, 1999 hadn't been too untidy. The game done and dusted, Jamie Cox acknowledged he'd played in four finals and never finished on the winning side.

Three of those anti-climaxes have been in Australia. But he counted Somerset's failure to overcome Gloucestershire as the biggest disappointment of them all. The game had had huge significance of bragging rights for anyone involved with West Country cricket. To lose against Gloucester was twice as painful for Jamie and the whole team.

'It hurt like nothing has hurt before, standing on the balcony watching the other side celebrate. I feel like I'm due that winning feeling.'

Beside me at Lord's that evening, Robert and Betty having gone 'into town' in search of additional 'fortification', Tubby breathed alcoholic fumes while casting the nod towards the deflated Cox huddled with his team-mates. He didn't mince his words. 'Australians are tough bastards. Somerset could do worse than stick with him for the time being.'

As Somerset entered the 'noughties' it was good someone wise listened, heartily sick, no doubt, of being reminded that the County hadn't won a trophy since sacking Viv Richards and Joel Garner and Ian Botham saying au revoir out of solidarity.

And as the curtain was pulled down on the 2000 season nothing looked like remotely changing. A couple of wins and ten draws earned Somerset 5th in County Championship, and 6th in Division 1 of the National League came courtesy of seven wins and eight losses. Unremarkable efforts. Yet those two competitions paled into insignificance in the light of Somerset's cataclysmic defeat at Southgate as they made a tail between the legs 4th round exit from the NatWest. I mean blimey, 58 all out! Broomfield, Laraman and Fraser ran through them like Lactulose syrup to undoubted sighs and inner compassion from the umpires, the former Somerset stalwarts Mervyn Kitchen and Ken Palmer. Only Keith Parsons and extras reached double figures. A different class, Middlesex had won by a gargantuan 165 run margin.

And then to cap they nearly lost Jamie Cox to an aquatic misadventure. On a team building mission Somerset went to Royal Naval Air Station at Yeovilton where groups of players were shown a helicopter cockpit and told to climb inside, take a seat and put on a seat belt it as hung suspended above a swimming pool. This was dunker drill.

It's a simple exercise. The cockpit's lowered and it fills up with water. As it does so you take a deep breath of air and hold it. Then you take you seat belt off, bust the window open, and everybody escapes in orderly fashion in about twenty seconds. So if, say, you're fifth in line it's sensible to ensure you've got air in your lungs whilst waiting your turn.

The first persons down were Coxy, Joe Tucker a young fast bowler and, a trio of

others. Matt Bulbeck was one of them. In '98 and again in '99 he had won the NBC Denis Compton Award presented annually to each county's 'Most Promising Young Player'.

Coxy did the window bit forgetting his seat belt was still cozily buckled. He panicked. Everybody behind him started going blue as they rapidly ran out of air. At the time Steffan Jones was up top gawping at the water and chatting nervously to the instructor who growled: 'they shouldn't be this long. There's something not right here.'

Suddenly there was nowt but pandemonium and splashes as a melee of instructors swimming around in the depths threw gasping bodies from the cockpit. Both the Zum skipper and his most promising young player just about lived. But, oh the trauma. Due to be part of the next group in, Steffan thought 'my God, what am I doing?'

The terror of nightmare showed in his haunted eyes as he spoke about what he then experienced. Given his Jona nickname I thought it prudent to keep any subjective witty analogy about the insides of a whale to myself as he spilled out more details. 'I felt the water coming up over my face and I took a gulp of air. But I took water with me, too. Bloomin' Nora, I had nothing. I had no air at all. Yes, I got out but it was a dreadful, dreadful experience and my worst Somerset memory.'

Dermot Reeve surfaced to announce his Somerset departure to concentrate on a safe media career. To Steffan the news came as a blow. He felt he owed Derm a lot. 'He saw something in me that others didn't and he encouraged me to concentrate on cricket, to work on my fitness and he gave me confidence in my own ability.' Whether that ability extended to holding a deep breath, I wasn't sure.

Trying to second-guess how Somerset's 2001 campaign would pan out gave cause to nibble fingernails. But there was a positive. The Head Coaching department would be left to Shine.

As I exited BBC Gloucestershire I knew that somewhere back in its bowels a sloppy researcher could have no idea of the memories his erroneous labelling had helped trigger.

Toughies and Postcards

'There is nothing more Australian than spending time in somebody else's country.'

Anon.

hat addict of Starbucks Strawberries and Cream Frappuccino Max Waller, ex Millfield School cricket captain and Zum leg break tweaky who'd yet to reduce a batsman to crutches, had last been observed in Taunton using his best prefect voice to tell off a whippersnapper for playing dent-dangerous car park cricket outside the County Ground's cricket academy.

Now the boot was on the other foot. It was Max who deserved a scolding. Frustratingly, he was well out of earshot across the Bass Strait. No point me shouting 'caution young man, 80% of those sweetie pies have Chlamydia' as he cuddled a koala in Adelaide.

Ostensibly Max was 'manning-up' out-wintering at the Darren Lehmann Cricket Academy, running around playing cricket in plus 40-degree heat whilst wearing black sweat inducing kit before jogging away on Outback tests of endurance-doubtless a case of Pom baiting pure and simple.

Surely the palava could have been averted. Max had done a week's road-tripping down the Gold Coast with Somerset team-mate Jack Leach whose hairline had receded to reveal a large, shiny forehead of the type popularly associated with noble and unworldly intellects. I just wondered if it crossed the said mind to have a quiet word to nip Max's attention grabbing Antipodean capers in the bud.

Although admittedly not quite the 'sun-baked dunny' a well-travelled mate of

mine had once described it as, taken as a whole, I had in the past observed Australia to be blooming elemental – red earth, hot air, infernos, floods, and dangerous creatures – supposing that over the years, the country's cricketers must have become fairly adept at living with such extreme adversity. For the likes of Somerset imports since Colin McCool – Greg Chappell, Steve Waugh, Cameron White and Justin Langer – facing up to missiles from Anderson, Finn and their England predecessors must have seemed a doddle.

Tazzie, though, Oz's equivalent of Zum's Steepholm was meant to have a kinder clime, more 'Mediterranean', perhaps making cricketing toughies the exception rather than the rule. In a topsy-turvy world that threatens to discombobulate, Somerset lies in the county of Wellington. Launceston and the Tamar Valley, home to the formidable Ricky 'Punter' Ponting is in Dorset. This is a land of kangaroo topped pizza and hardhead ducks, where yellow-tailed black cockatoos feed on a diet of wood-boring grubs that, if left to their own devices, might endanger a batman's willow. It was here, in 1851, with only four balls permitted per over, that the first first-class game of cricket in Australia was ever played. Without boundaries, and with no time limit, it took place upon a racecourse. And where in 1988 a certain Ian Botham of Queensland trashed a dressing room with the help of a badly behaved Dennis Lillee.

On hearing I was to pootle about Tasmania for a while, Nick Compton had offered me a crumb of comfort. 'Tazzie's nice. My buddies who've been say it's great.'

However, my wife Ali and I considered Australia's 'Island State' more 'grate' than 'great' as we hit the 'frog and toad' and high-tailed it north out of Hobart, astonished at local attitude arising out of Ali announcing 'I don't really do bush fires'. A shiela had responded: 'Oh, that's so cute.'

Agreeing with my wife that the lady could jolly well keep her darling conflagrations, escape offered us the excuse for a purposeful road trip. Sensing the irony we set the car's satnav for Burnie.

I felt compelled to discover the influences that had touched Jamie Cox's character. I mean, the former Tasmania skipper and Australian Test team selector, notwithstanding his role in the West Country cricket, was hardly a bushwacker. Some went so far as to say he was 'incredible'. His everyday appearance was always pristine – clean-shaven, immaculate coif, and starched upturned collar on his white cricket shirt. Always looking after his kit, this tidy methodical person was a very well organized unit.

Earning the respect of people to follow him as an effective leader, he was extremely unlucky that he never wore the 'baggy green' due to the number of exceptional players, including Langer, about during the era of his pomp. But he never showed that frustration, not once whilst scoring 18,614 first-class runs in a

19-year career that ended in 2005. He just really enjoyed playing the game and living by his own performances, scoring everything between backward point and extra cover off the front foot and off the back foot. He churned out his runs and expected everyone else to follow suit.

Gaining everyone's respect is essential to a leader, but all good captains like to fit in as a team-mate as well. A true pro, Coxy mixed it with the boys when he had to. And his runs at the top of the order set up Somerset innings nicely. Batting, he maintained, required clear plans and he tried to get the lads to make them decently.

And the way he used to deport himself one can see today mirrored in people like James Hildreth. When he first came onto the scene Jamie was Hildy's captain, and those things have rubbed off. Being such a positive influence led the senior players, too, to follow Jamie through thick and thin, even when his very good cricket brain might have got it wrong. Such as putting Gloucester into bat after winning the '99 C&G Final toss.

Coxy was quite happy even when there were strong personalities in the changing room to stand up them. Of course players could voice their initial thoughts but he'd stubbornly say 'no, this is the way we're going to do things' if he believed it was in the best interests of the team. There was no confrontation. The team would just unite and follow him. Or as Dermot Reeve might have said: 'crack on'.

From the Bass Highway the sea was never far distant. The scenery passing beside the bonnet was of undulating countryside and painted wood slat homesteads. Rustic post and wire fencing keeping cows in browned grassy fields and 4 x 4 Japanese pickups driven by adventurous mullet-cropped, cashed-up bogans – the urban rednecks- out. Yet, under a wisp-cloud sky, there seemed a distinct lack of cricket pitches.

The large container port town, the first goal on our hasty itinerary, was a must see. A high school boy here broke the all-schools batting record for Australian school cricket, previously held by Bill Lawry. That boy was Jamie Cox and, by extraordinary coincidence, Ali and I discovered his hangout in the town's suburbs – a Somerset where the two-storey, flat roofed brick post office wouldn't look amiss on the A38 Bristol Road between Bridgwater and Dunball.

Not normally one prone to exaggeration Ali giggled: 'we're in Lilliput! Somerset Down Under is tiddlier than Wiveliscombe, but much tidier.'

In truth it was the quintessence of Jamie. Smooth surfaced parking lots, smart bungalows, clipped cypress trees and immaculately mown verges bordered the gentle gradient of Falmouth Street's wide thoroughfare. Down at the bottom beside the sea was the Esplanade and Somerset Strikers Cricket Club. The whole

caboodle must have provided the sub-conscious of Jamie's salad days a wonderful sense of compass in the years to come as he flourished professionally.

Like other Aussie cricketers he was very proud of his heritage – proud of the people who have gone before. In equal measure Jamie Cox loved the Somerset he found in England's West Country – the County Cricket Club, the area, the people – to a point of passion. Being club captain wasn't just a job, it seemed a calling.

However, there was another side to the man immortalised within the Tasmanian community, that of a cricket writer and, quite possibly, a clairvoyant.

During his time as a player, his *Postcards* series appeared in various newspapers. On Thursday 29th March 2001 in the warm-up to the English season he wrote: 'Hot tip – Somerset to win a trophy in England this year. Reasonable odds will be available for those willing and allowed to have a punt but, after two solid and threatening years, I think this could be the year of the Sabres!'

For a county not having won a pheasant's feather in 18 years this was fighting talk from a Somerset skipper with something of a burning desire. Once back in Blighty, I decided, I'd chat to someone in the know about the momentous events that followed during a first year for new coach Kevin Shine. 'Derm' had vacated to concentrate on nattering into a commentary box microphone.

FIVE

Polishing Silver

'If winning isn't everything, why do they keep score?'

Vincent Lombardi.

Heavens, it wasn't apocryphal that the county proud manager of the local Co-op had ordered in extra boxes of Cox apples, inadvertently adding to the pink ladies among the town's Methodists in that year of chasing Foxes, and the first in two consecutive seasons of Tyke tussles.

On the hunt for 2001 memories the very chap I was looking for was twiddling a couple of bats in his daily place of work, an elegant straight chip away from the middle where I'd most recently watched him entertain as a Unicorn. Eight seasons it took him to earn his county cap as a bits-and-pieces player, but by the early 'noughties' he matured and grew into what *Guardian* journalist John Collis called 'a Somerset giant'. Given the confines of his current office there was certainly the illusion of this being true.

Tucked away at the back of the Old Pavilion, the gloomy, airless back room of the *County Sports* shop was dominated by an insistent telephone, a battered metal filing cabinet and a desk so cluttered there was hardly room for my Molskine notebook. A small chair, its seat sagged from the weight of visiting bottoms plonked upon it over the years, protested my restless girth. The heating was definitely on too high.

As instinctive to my discomfort as to the spin in a 'wrong'un', Keith Parsons, 'Pars' to his mates, stretched courteously to turn it off. I had never imagined him as an office wallah. As a youngster his Taunton St Andrews club teammates had nicknamed him 'Orv' after 'Orville the Duck' though this was more to do with his

manner of walking than any lack of batting prowess. Yet seeing him now he seemed akin to a Tone mallard at silly point – a tad wary and out of place.

Across town in Vivary Park the yellow trumpet heads of cultivated King Alfreds, the Trescothicks of the daffodil world, were in full bloom. However, the ancient warrior monarch is, perhaps, better remembered by the inspirational nature of the Wyvern beast upon his heraldic banner that flew from castle ramparts than by any floral tribute.

Centuries later the emblem fluttering from a pole or stitched into Somerset's cricket apparel continues to galvanize. And none more than the soul who emerged from Taunton's Castle – that's to say Castle School, the co-educational secondary. I thought it appropriate, given the word 'Wyvern' derives from the French *guivre* meaning viper, that when called upon in an hour of need Keith would try his valiant damnedest to smite leather with venom.

During his seventeen seasons at his beloved Somerset he had matched the achievements of the knightly Botham, scoring 5,000 runs and taking 100 wickets in both four-day and one-day cricket. Of all those seasons '01 stood out for Keith like a beacon light.

I raised the topic of the *Postcard* and asked Keith's opinion of its scribbler. 'Jamie Cox? He was just a typical hard-nosed Aussie.' Now, this wasn't quite the blunt assessment of his former skipper I was expecting. Especially when '01, did indeed, turn out to be the year of the 'Sabres'.

My hope for a tad more insight was rewarded by Keith breaking the pregnant silence by adding: 'But Coxy was a super bloke. And backed it up with a stack load of runs as well.'

Under his guidance in '01 Somerset were motivated into being the best they could be. They had a great run in the Championship. A late run. Even the diehard optimist believed they were never going to win it, but towards the back end they were breathing down Yorkshire's neck. Vic Marks, who'd once been in the thick of the *Glory Years* and labelled by *Wisden* editor, Matthew Engel, as 'a mild, nervy, self-deprecating farm boy with an Oxford degree and no enemies' spoke on behalf of the hierarchy when he remarked 'things have become rather exciting again here.'

The bowling that year had been outstanding but, in all fairness, so was the batting. In trying to find the point when Somerset threw down the gauntlet to Yorkshire one had to look to Bath and drawing of willow blades in June. Both sides only got to bat once in something of a stalemate on a paradisiacal pitch.

The first two days belonged to the Wonder of Walney. Mike Burns in at 3 had the cricket anoraks reaching for the record books with a marathon double century.

Before he inadvertently tried to sweep and limply looped Middlebrook gently to wicky Blakey, the one-time Barrow shipyard fitter – better known for his cracking, aggressive style at the crease – had, on this occasion, been riveting in other ways. He faced 367 deliveries in a seven-and-three-quarter hour knock, hitting 28 fours and a six as Zum reached a first innings total of 553 for 5 declared, which was marginally upstaged by the Tykes 589 for a similar loss of wickets before rain brought a merciful release for the bowlers.

However, Burns' score was the highest ever by a Somerset batsman against Yorkshire, eclipsing the 217 made by Viv Richards at Harrogate in 1975 and it remains the biggest total made by a Somerset batsman at Bath, and also the highest score ever by a Cumbrian in First Class cricket.

Trencherman Mark Lathwell had held the high score record at Bath since making 206 in 1994, and he too joined the latest run-feast with a knock of brilliance. He began batting at 11.25 and had reached a breathtaking 98 at lunch when cruelly Jamie Cox made a presumably pre-arranged declaration with Somerset on 553 for five.

In a way Mark had only himself to blame for not getting his hundred, perhaps by piercing the field with a replica of the sweet cuts he had been showing off throughout the morning, or even a slog, like the one moving him past 50 that landed on the roof of the Friends of Bath tent, reportedly causing a 'ripple of Chardonnay'. However, with five minutes to go before the interval he went down on one knee and launched Middlebrook for six. The immaculate connection cleared the leg side marquees and inconveniently hid under a car on the rugby ground. Vital minutes were lost that would have allowed another over and the chance to clip the couple of runs needed for his century. However, toughie Cox, to a chorus of groans, closed the innings.

Looking across the desk to Keith I mentioned that I'd been one of the groaners.

He failed to criticise Cox for the timing of the declaration. Probably, it wasn't politic. Instead, he applauded Lathwell. 'Oh, some of the innings 'Trough' played! I think I put on 80 with him at Kent in a rain affected one-dayer and I only got 5 of them. We went off for rain and came back out and decided we had seven or eight overs left and he just smashed it everywhere. He could just do that to any class of bowling – it was fantastic.

'And he's a lovely bloke,' I said, adding 'I interviewed him in the 1990s on the Atkinson pavilion balcony. Came across as someone content with their own company.'

Keith nodded. 'One place we stayed at in the Midlands there was a fishing pond and he went out there and fished all night. His type of evening was loaf of bread

and a ready roasted chicken in his room where he'd sit and watch telly. He'd do his own little things in his own quirky little way. He probably didn't enjoy the hype and the media of international cricket. But had he taken to it, I think he would have had a long career.

'If you count Marcus (Trescothick) aside, I think, Mark was as good an English player that I've played with. He could turn a game on the toss of a coin, really. It's an old cliché but he's someone that you'd be here at eleven o'clock to watch if he was opening the batting. He played some amazing shots and has his own technique. Yer, pity he didn't get that hundred at Bath.'

For 'Burnsy', on the other hand, the match brought a further statistic of delight. His 221 beat his previous best knock of 160 against Oxford University in the first April of the new millennium. He expressed his relief to a hack from Cumbria's *News & Star*. 'The lads have been giving me dreadful stick because my best total came against the students and it's a relief to have knocked that statistic out of the record books.' That said, his score against the students' remains the earliest century recorded in an English county season.

Come the third day in Bath Somerset suffered a casualty. A fleshy prang caused by a zealous piece of fielding gave Mike Burns further opportunity to show his mettle.

Cox, after an altercation with an unforgiving boundary board, had broken his thumb, forcing him to relinquish short-term command when a week later Somerset set off to the Isle of Ely and the Fenlands of March to begin their C&G campaign. Entering at the third round, Burnsy led for the first time with Rob Turner as his second in command and fate smiled a winning start. A Mark Lathwell century and a 4-wicket cluster from the Suffolk punch Jamie Grove, in a rare first-team appearance, put paid to plucky Cambridgeshire.

The win earned a home tie against Glamorgan. This transpired to be relatively stress free, although Matthew Maynard making it into the 'nineties' gave the Welshmen dignity. Somerset achieved victory still having the better part of 8 overs left in the locker, largely due to Trescothick's ninety minute stay at the crease, cracking 20 boundary fours in his 121 off 83 balls.

A trip to Canterbury then ensued for the quarter-final.

Batting first after winning the toss the Somerset effort was solid without being exceptional. Blackwell accumulated a half-ton in almost as many balls and Burns was cautious in his 71.

However, Somerset's end tally of 263 was beyond Kent. Pars disposed of the middle order of Symonds, Ealham and Nixon, and when Steffan Jones, off his own bowling, ran out Wellington born Zum discard Ben Trott Somerset were in

the semi-finals by a margin of 52 runs.

July melded into August, and as it did so a sense of anticipation grew around the County Ground. In a tie billed by the press as a battle between England's Trescothick and Knight, Warwickshire, skippered by Mike Powell and coached by Bob Woolmer, stood between Somerset and another day out at Lord's.

An hour after the toss Cox must have wondered whether that trip would happen, and certainly would have done after Trescothick was comprehensively outduelled. After putting the visitors in under a weepy grey sky the tide of events seemed to go in a remarkably similar fashion to the '99 final.

Obviously cunning plans were discussed. The job of Andy Caddick and Richard Johnson was to bowl short to the openers Nick Knight and, boyishly thin Tavaré lookalike, Mark Wagh. From where I sat, Caddick interpreted Plan A as a need to decapitate. Half a dozen chords of chin music filled his first two overs. Knight bobbed and weaved. Then weaved when he should have bobbed and was floored by a half-lengther. The sound of the ball cannoning off his helmet reverberated around the ground, giving rise to the first sing-song 'Somerset-la-la-la'. Umpire Barrie Leadbeater felt the need to have a quiet word with Captain Cox. Umpire Mervyn Kitchen tried but failed miserably to suppress a giggle.

Woozily Knight dusted himself down, gritted his teeth, and then, on three, edged. Rob Turner, surprisingly agile for such a tall man, plunged to claim the catch. Third umpire Mark Benson ruled the ball hadn't carried raising further debate about the efficacy of TV replays and blessed cameras foreshortening images. Plan A had nearly worked but not quite. To his credit Knight began a common sense game of tip and scoot and, with partner Wagh on-driving beautifully, the pair went on to construct a foundation Barratt would have been proud of with a first-wicket stand of 101.

Step up Keith Parsons and Mike Burns for Plan B. Medium pace was now the way to go. And hurrah, it worked. Wagh was the first to depart. A mistimed drive saw Keith pull off a stunner – a one-handed return catch almost a pitch away. The partisans erupted. Cider was spilt.

Keith gave me a wistful smile as I reminded him of the game changing moment.

Taking pace off the ball, he and Burnsy had turned the tide. Four wickets fell for 52 off 13 overs. And it was Keith who took the scalp of Knight, skittled as he swiped across the line. Cue more spilt cider. And it was left largely to Michael Powell, to add 70 inelegant, invaluable runs with Trevor Penney.

The day, however, would belong to another Keith, Keith Dutch. The wily off-spinner, released by Middlesex at the end of the previous season, had been rather

surplus to requirements at Taunton that day until called upon to fling himself full-length to snaffle a rasping David Hemp cut. He achieved even greater heroics with his willow when Somerset set about the task of reeling in 228 which, given Warwickshire's start, pundits thought was 30 or 40 runs short.

The Midlanders took the field without their groggy Knight, whisked to Musgrove hospital as a precaution responsibility of best all-round fielder was handed to Penney whose reputation lay in the runs he saved rather than those he made. And for the locals watching he turned out to be a rather bad Penney.

If Zum had a simple Plan C to go out there and knock off the runs, the distraught cry of 'Holy Mother of God!' from my River Stand neighbour announced it heading for the window as Bears jumped and hugged like a bunch of old school Tone Vale lunatics. Five minutes after Trescothick had pulled Dougie Brown for four in the Scot's first over Somerset were alarmingly 6 for 3. Marcus lost his off stump to Brown. Bowler fended off Neil Carter's second ball to the said Penney. And Burnsy unable to cope with a Brown brute made it a Penney dreadful.

Despite the 'Somerset-la-la-las' becoming audibly desultory, the gurt Taunton crowd still oozed a little trust as Captain Cox led a partial recovery. However, Zum carelessly slid to 130 for six after Cox and Ian Blackwell both failed to convert good starts. Keith, too, suffered similarly, trapped almost plumb in front by Brummie Mohamed Sheikh. Mervyn Kitchen doing his level best to be impartial gave the benefit of the only ell bee of the match. Now there really was trouble, but nil desperandum.

Noting the thirty-somethings and a lack of spring chickens in the side the *Guardian's* Paul Weaver had described Somerset as 'long in batting and long in tooth' But with age comes the wisdom that Taunton was a fast-scoring ground. With the required rate a little over five an over all that needed to be done was to ensure that it didn't creep up to a run a ball while keeping their precious remaining wickets intact. And thanks to Dutch and Turner, this Zum did.

With 61 not out from 54 balls, including 10 boundaries Dutch won man of the match. Turner contributed 42 not out. Between them they put on 100 in 86 balls and the home side pootled home with four overs in hand.

Dutch revelled in glory. 'This has to be the best time in my life. It feels great to be going back to Lord's after spending my career at Middlesex, especially after not cutting it there. When I left Middlesex I felt that they hadn't given me enough opportunities. But those they did give me I didn't take. I decided I wanted just one year to prove myself.

'The difference here is the confidence I've been given by everyone. For the first time I'm playing regularly, week in week out, and I'm a much better cricketer as a result.'

The lad spoke true. His six for 40 had helped Zum to a vital win over Northamptonshire in Norwich Union League when they were battling to avoid relegation. And in the championship challenge his contribution was in no way small either, taking 35 wickets and averaging 29.44.

More than an hour after Somerset's win, after the delirium had subsided with the setting sun and the last stragglers wobbled home to savour what was to come, Captain Cox delivered the news the whole county had been waiting for: he would return in 2002.

It must have felt a little like a blessing as the ground staff watered the square.

The news that he was about to start a family had fuelled speculation that he was about to return to Tasmania. 'Next year,' he said, 'I will have a young baby with me. But I want to come back and give it a really good crack.'

At the time I hoped he wasn't taking about the baby.

Jamie went on to assure all listeners that he wanted to make up for his personal disappointment in not scoring a century at any point in the season. As it was the Championship would remain a chimera. The Tykes had the top spot, although proper squeezed and losing more games than Zum who'd come a wonderful second with a willing workhorse. For his 59 championship wickets Steffan Jones sent down 560 overs, earning the title the 'Welsh bison' from Kevin Shine. Sussex's James Kirtley was the only seamer in the country to bowl more.

Yorkshire, too, had got the wood over Somerset in the quarter-final of the Benson & Hedges. Defeat here led to a slight changing room bust up. 'Michael Vaughan got a hundred and we got hammered,' summed up Steffan who as normal had put his body through extremes of effort. 'I was obviously exhausted and the boys went and asked whether we could play touch rugby. I went ballistic and shouted: "how can you have energy to play touch rugby? If you gave everything in that game you wouldn't have any energy." And Noddy (Rob Turner) pissed up and said something. So we were going at each other. I had to be pulled back by Darren Veness, the strength and conditioning coach, and Rob Turner had to be pulled back by Kevin Shine. The rest of the boys were excited and yelling: "hold them back! Hold them back!' Afterwards Noddy and I went into the physio room and sorted it out. But honestly it was a storm in a tea cup, we really were a family.'

Thanks to Dutch courage against Kent, however, 'the family' did at least have something greatly positive to celebrate.

Following an unbothered wait of twenty-four hours the name of their Lord's opposition was learned. At a damp Grace Road, Leicestershire finally annihilated Lancashire over two days in-between the cloudbursts. Scott Boswell tweaked out

the Red Rose top order cheaply, returning figures of 4 for 44, as the hosts failed to put 200 on the board before Shahid Afridi, in a wondrous slogathon, bludgeoned 95 off 58 deliveries bringing the Foxes home with more than 20 overs to spare.

I posed Keith Parsons the question whether the final was his most memorable match.

'Had to be,' he replied, his eyes suddenly shining. More than a dozen years on, the emotion remained clear to see. It was something he'd dreamed about since family weekends of watching his dad play back in times of Saturday West Somerset League games and old fashion friendlies on a Sunday. Then Keith and his twin brother Kevin would occupy themselves with a bat and ball on the side of the pitch. Eventually, aged of nine, they'd stick their kit in the car just in case someone didn't turn up. And within a year an opportunity presented itself. The twins found themselves turning out for Taunton St Andrews at Exeter St. Thomas. 'I fielded at fine leg and third man and jogged from one end to the other. We were bred in quite early,' Keith recalled.

'But Man of the Match in '01 is what, in a way, I'll be remembered for, I think. The Final was a massive occasion for us.'

Every Somerset follower, I'm sure, would agree. Before that first day of September Somerset hadn't won a trophy since 1983. However, coach Kevin Shine was optimistic before the start of play. He felt that Somerset's two victories over Leicestershire in the Norwich Union League earlier in the summer had given his side the psychological edge. 'Shahid Afridi came off against us in both matches,' he said, 'but that also gave us time to have a look at him. We have a plan for him. And he hasn't faced Andrew Caddick or Richard Johnson yet.'

Then he added the proverbial get out clause, just in case, that the Pakistani was 'such a sensational player that he could come off whatever we do.' Somerset were definitely worried about Mister Afridi.

In amongst thousands of Somerset folk and less vocal bands of Leicester supporters my two pubescent sons, who'd immersed themselves in the summer game worryingly late, could relish their first family outing to the 'home of cricket'. Each believed Trescothick to be a minor deity and neither could comprehend any other result that a glorious Somerset triumph. At the toss under clear London skies I just crossed my fingers and toes and tried to push '99, not to mention '67 and '78, to the back of my mind. The flicked coin spun its rotations of luck and upon landing declared Captain Cox having the initial success. And hurrah, he wasn't going to make the mistake he did against Gloucester on this particular daunting, tension-soaked occasion. This time 'Tresco' and Bowler were going to have first dip. The pitch was as flat as a pancake, so it was said, and Coxy decided to set the pace of the game from the middle.

Leicester skipped onto the field to a sea of noise that rose like a seventh wave when Zum's opening pair appeared and strode purposefully towards their respective creases shadow batting an array of strokes.

And at the start, Trescothick batted as if he was going to make the final his own. Scott Boswell as a surprise choice of opening bowler soon put that idea to bed as if to emphasize the traditional finale of the season is nowt but a day of sweaty palms.

By all accounts 'Bozzy' was a gutsy Tyke, a bright man and graduate of 'Wolly Poly' that's to say Wolverhampton University. He had opened the bowling with Steffan Jones for British Universities and in 1996 had attended Dennis Lillee's Madras Pace Foundation. Yet none of this experience was a help to him when, in the words of an *Observer* correspondent, 'he got the cricketing equivalent of the yips'.

'His bowling was just funny,' Steffan observed putting his bowling coach's hat on and discussing the bloke he's known for a long time. 'It was poor coaching to be fair. They let him go because he managed to get wickets because they were caught down the leg side. After the semi-final Leicester had offered him a new three-year contract. "Oh, that's wonderful," he'd said, "I'll sign it after the final."

Bozzy only bowled a couple of overs, but sadly this constituted 21 balls. A low arm and open chest caused havoc, re-inventing the concept of moving the ball away from the bat. In his second over he propelled eight wides causing further *Observer* lament that it was 'probably the poorest over seen at Lord's since men in top hats used to lob them'.

Sighing heavily, Steffan remembered. 'We were on the Lord's balcony. Soon as the first went wide we were like "that's quite funny ha ha ha". Then three of them went and after the third one we thought: "come on now, just get one straight." I felt sorry for him. You don't like to be taking the micky out of someone who in your profession is struggling a bit. We were hoping he'd get off, hopefully compose himself and come back. Just for his sake really.'

Boswell tried everything. He tried holding the ball across the seam; he tried bowling around the wicket; beads of sweat flooded from his forehead and seemed to terminate in his right hand. However hard he tried he could not get the damn sphere to land on the famously sloping cut strip.

'The thing is,' Steffan Jones told me sagely, 'when you face someone like that there is always one ball he might get right. And on the balcony we were thinking "oh, please don't get one jaffa and get Trescothick out". But he did get one straight and Marcus hit him for four. So it was like "Oh bless him. Why not just go off?"'

Sometime during 2012 Steffan caught up him again with Bozzy. Time had healed him a little. Philosophical, he admitted having had a struggle bowling to left handers. His slingy action meant he couldn't get his line because the ball went away. And obviously with Trescothick being the best left-hander in the country if not the world he just got so tense.

'Keeping our keeper supple are yer?' taunted a running fox sun hat.

'Wide 'e bovver!' heckled a load of hair two rows further down.

Foxes skipper Vince Wells put Bozzy out to pasture at third man where he dived despairingly in an attempt to prevent Trescothick glancing a boundary. Poignantly all he managed to do was gouge out the biggest divot in the world, leaving a hole that wasn't quite big enough to swallow him up.

By contrast Trescothick had looked in top form. Every shot played was middled, his three boundaries making my sons cheer to the top of their lungs. Then, damn it, he went and daftly swiped lazily to leg, or to give him the benefit of the doubt, he just mistimed an attempted pull. There was no prizes for guessing that it was Afridi who took the catch scampering back from mid-on, gifting Tresco's new England team-mate James Ormond the first wicket.

It was the signal to send the West Countrymen into their shell. After 15 overs – the last of them being a Vince Wells maiden of wobbly-dobblies – Somerset were 60 for one. And, of course, they had Bozzy to thank for 23 of those. Undeniably strangled they were on the back foot. And things got worse seven runs later with the introduction of Afridi's fizzing wrist-spinners. They don't spin much but their trajectory was deceptive. He put paid to Bowler, pranging the veteran's stumps off an inside edge.

New batsman Ian Blackwell responded by launching Afridi for six over a shortened boundary at mid-wicket. When 'Blackie' perished attempting a similar shot four overs later, timbers again rearranged by Afridi, as he attempted to hit a googly over the top, Zum became kamikaze. Jamie Cox followed in his next over in identical fashion.

Fifteen overs from home, Somerset were 168 for four – a meagre 4.8 an over – with Michael Burns on 19 and Keith Parsons on six.

And when Burnsy picked out Darren Maddy to take a beetling catch in the deep leaving Zum on 176 for five the advantage lay firmly with Leicester. Bozzy's antics were now placed firmly at the back of the mind.

'We're going to lose, aren't we Dad?' said my youngest, glumly.

'Don't think like that just yet,' I soothed. 'Pars is still there. Turner can tonk it. And if all else fails Steffan can hit a long ball.'

But as it transpired Steffan wasn't needed. Instead Keith Parsons and Rob Turner developed Zum's biggest partnership of the match that wrested the momentum. Pushing the ball around effectively to begin with, keeping the scoreboard ticking over, the duo grew in confidence moving past 200 as they set about the final 10 overs.

Keith smote three fours to find his range then, in the 48th over, he hit Phil 'Daffy' DeFreitas for a huge six, disturbing those members in the Allen Stand who might have been facing the bar at the time. It was the sort of stroke Afridi might have been proud of. And there were a couple more to come. From the second last ball of their innings, he wellied another big six, this time to the Tavern side, bringing up his own 50. For good measure, he put Daffy's final delivery over the ropes as well, and now Somerset had a total to play with. The Foxes had been left a chase of 272 at a run rate of 5.42 runs per over.

'Me and Rob putting on ninety-five in the last few overs was quite key,' said Keith ignoring the telephone ringing on the office desk. 'And hitting the last couple of balls out of the ground was special. We were still twenty runs short but it was all about momentum. There was a buzz about the dressing room with what we'd achieved.

And obviously we went out after the break to face Afridi opening their innings. Fair to say his batting was predictable.'

The ball briefly exploded in every direction except that anticipated. Fortunately for Somerset he only scored 20, coming and went going so quickly that after-lunch stragglers missed one of the season's craziest innings.

Andy Caddick bowled a maiden to Trevor Ward – the highlight of which was Afridi almost running himself out first ball – then the mania began. With a huge flourish Afridi top-edge Richard Johnson's first ball from the pavilion end. Somehow it looped to safety and set the tone of his 10-ball stay.

Upon getting another crack at Johnson, he larruped a full-toss into the Tavern multitude then, making room to leg, deliberately sliced him to third man. A similar slap found the point boundary. Then, predetermined now for assault, Afridi swung lustily again, this time sending the ball rocketing to the heavens and the tears of Leicester angels. It was one of the highest skiers ever seen at Lord's.

As Rob Turner circled, his eyes on the descent and time a-plenty to ponder the consequences of a drop, the slip cordon fell over themselves getting the hell out of his way.

Steffan, who was at mid-on, reminisced on his thoughts during those momentous seconds. 'We'd played Leicestershire twice before in one day games during the season and I opened the bowling twice and I got him out once. But he did some damage twice. He was dropped a few times at the game at Taunton.

'When the ball went up, I thought "oh please catch it 'cos I'm not going to have to bowl to him. And the moment the ball plugged safely in Noddy's gloves Afridi was halfway back to the pavilion while I went round and round the stumps about five times just following Jono (Richard Johnson). I got a bit giddy.'

Such happy outcome had been cause for my sons to bounce up and down like a pair of mazed hares, early doom and gloom evaporated. The running fox sun hat, however, looked anguished.

The pivotal moment of the game had offered itself and from that moment on Zum knew the game was theirs although Pars' dismissal of the fluent Trevor Ward and the dangerous Vince Wells were timely.

'It's what, in a way, I'll be remembered for, I think,' Keith smiled. 'The Final was a massive occasion for us. So whilst Boswell tried to hog the limelight with his thirteen-ball over, hopefully it'll still be remembered as my match.

'We were always ahead of the game. They'd slog a few and we'd get another wicket. We knew from about ten overs out that they weren't going to get them. That was just an extraordinary atmosphere – with a packed house at Lord's and, obviously, knowing that we were that close. And when Steffan got Bozzy out at the end … well, that was amazing.'

When Boswell came into bat there was the biggest noise. It was massive with shouts of 'Bring on the Bozzy!' As good as any death bowler in the country and generating 90 m.p.h. Steffan, Somerset's most successful bowler that day, backed his own skills. 'We passed as he was coming down,' said Steffan, 'and I went to smile 'cos he was a broken man.' The coup de grâce took four balls. Bails flying, Bozzy's wicket was broken, too.

And yet the heart of the unlucky Boswell hadn't finished bleeding. A last ignominy awaited him upon his return to a sombre Leicester dressing room. His contract was ripped up, effectively ending his cricketing career.

Not that this was in Somerset minds. 'I just remember Jamie Cox jumping on my back. It was brilliant,' relived Steffan clenching his fist at the memory, before he went on to tell me about Somerset's lap of honour.

'I remember doing a lap and just running off into the crowd to see my wife and my parents and stuff. And as we came round the other side by the pavilion I ran

off somewhere else and a TV camera followed me, but all I was doing was going to pick up my water bottle. I turned round and there was a camera there. "I'm only getting my water bottle," I said. And they must have thought, oh great TV that one. The best bit was going back up the changing rooms to see the coaches and the staff and twelfth, thirteenth and fourteenth men.'

Keith Parsons picked up the day's remaining honour. 'I do recall the Somerset fans going a little potty, my sons and I included,' I said to him. 'And there was you being awarded Man of the Match. 60 runs, including the three sixes, and also those two wickets was a good day out.'

Keith looked bashful. 'I think that was something I'd been aiming for, but hadn't expected until we got off the field and someone said: "you've got to get it". So I thought well, looking around, yep maybe I will.

'Derm was on the mike at the ground so it was pretty special. Derm was a good influence on me. He gave me a lot of opportunity here.'

I think Keith was so wrapped in memory that he missed my sudden quizzical frown. However, I wasn't going to go down the road of asking about 'influences'. Not now that Derm had admitted to a cocaine addiction, and had used the drug prior to commentating on the 2004 first Test between England and New Zealand at blooming Lord's and duly quit Channel Four.

'… for him to be announcing the award was a good moment,' Keith continued to reflect. From a selfish point of view that's what I'll look back on as one of the best days.'

'Did you celebrate with a cider?' I asked.

Keith laughed. 'There was no cider afterwards, but we had a few.'

Steffan had had difficulty in elucidating further. 'We celebrated for two hours after the game. What happened in the night is still a blur.'

'We always knew how to enjoy a victory,' Keith grinned. 'That was a key part. I know the professional game has changed now. But we enjoyed the good times, and when we were going well we enjoyed it.'

And there was no reason not to, what with polishing silver, declaring an 18-year famine over, and coming second in the Championship for the first time. Indeed, the BBC's Simon Mann eulogized: 'for Somerset this was, quite simply, the best season in their history'.

That it transpired to be so was remarkable. Andy Caddick was available for only

two championship matches although his 18 wickets ensured that Somerset won them both. Marcus Trescothick's role was less influential. He played in three games, scoring 216 runs in four innings. Both had more involvement in their one-day success but Somerset were able to compensate for their unavailability through a strong, all-round team effort, supported by shrewd signings.

Zum's player of the season went to the magnificent Richard Johnson. He had been brought in specifically as cover for Caddick. Only debatably was he the pick of the pace bowlers, finishing with 62 wickets. However, he did earn a call-up to the England Test squad.

Unsurprisingly the seasonal revolving doors of county cricket were little noticed as Jamie Gove, an unsung Caddick cover, quietly made his exit. Coming the other way were the Francis brothers, Simon and his younger sibling John, snaffled from the Hogs.

The acquisitions augured well, the Wyvern beast fluttered proudly in autumn winds, and in the local Co-op, boxes of Cox apples were on reorder. However, the manner in which things would begin to unravel meant Somerset's glow of success and optimism revealed itself as fleeting light.

CHELTENHAM & GLOUCESTER TROPHY FINAL 2001
Leicestershire v Somerset
Lord's
1st September 2001

Umpires B Dudleston and G Sharp
TV umpire RA White

Somerset won the toss and chose to bat.

Somerset innings		R	M	B	4s	6s	SR
ME Trescothick	c Shahid Afridi b Ormond	18	29	18	3	0	100.00
PD Bowler	b Shahid Afridi	42	107	85	6	0	49.41
J Cox*	b Shahid Afridi	44	98	64	4	0	68.75
ID Blackwell	b Shahid Afridi	15	12	16	1	1	93.75
M Burns	c Maddy b Wells	21	24	23	1	0	91.30
KA Parsons	not out	60	69	52	3	3	115.38
RJ Turner†	not out	37	51	42	2	0	88.09
Extras	(lb 19, w 15)	34					
Total	(5 wickets; 50 overs)	271					

Did not bat: KP Dutch, RL Johnson, AR Caddick, PS Jones.

Fall of wickets 1-40 (Trescothick), 2-107 (Bowler), 3-132 (Blackwell), 4-149 (Cox), 5-176 (Burns)

Bowling	O	M	R	W	Econ	
J Ormond	10	2	38	1	3.80	(2w)
SAJ Boswell	2	0	23	0	11.50	(9w)
PAJ DeFreitas	10	1	57	0	5.70	(2w)
VJ Wells	10	1	40	1	4.00	
DL Maddy	8	0	47	0	5.87	(1w)
Shahid Afridi	10	0	47	3	4.70	(1w)

Leicestershire innings		R	M	B	4s	6s	SR
TR Ward	b Parsons	54	80	65	10	0	83.07
Shahid Afridi	c †Turner b Johnson	20	13	10	3	0	200.00
DL Maddy	c & b Dutch	49	106	71	3	0	69.01
VJ Wells*	c †Turner b Parsons	3	5	8	0	0	37.50
BF Smith	c Trescothick b Dutch	15	16	18	1	0	83.33
DI Stevens	lbw b Jones	23	33	32	1	0	71.87
ND Burns†	c †Turner b Jones	6	9	9	1	0	66.66
A Habib	c Dutch b Blackwell	15	23	19	1	0	78.94
PAJ DeFreitas	b Johnson	14	34	23	1	0	60.86
J Ormond	not out	18	24	18	1	1	100.00
SAJ Boswell	b Jones	2	5	4	0	0	50.00
Extras	(lb 3, w 2, nb 6)	11					
Total	(all out; 45.4 overs)	230					

Fall of wickets 1-20 (Shahid Afridi), 2-105 (Ward), 3-111 (Wells), 4-142 (Smith), 5-156 (Maddy), 6-171 (Burns), 7-182 (Stevens), 8-194 (Habib), 9-225 (DeFreitas), 10-230 (Boswell)

Bowling	O	M	R	W	Econ	
AR Caddick	10	2	33	0	3.30	(2nb)
RL Johnson	8	0	39	2	4.87	(2w)
PS Jones	7.4	0	40	3	5.21	
KA Parsons	6	0	40	2	6.66	(1nb)
KP Dutch	10	0	50	2	5.00	
ID Blackwell	4	0	25	1	6.25	

Somerset won by 41 runs.

Man of the match: KA Parsons.

SIX

Hops and Drop

'Winning takes talent, to repeat takes character.'

John Wooden.

A tad shy of thirty, the self-reliant Welsh bison built a gym in the garage of his Taunton home. There he spent his winter fanatically improving his fitness with three sessions a day of muscle bulking sweated effort drawing upon javelin and baseball techniques. On Christmas Day he did allow himself a concession. He cut his periods of devoted activity to two. With the flowering of 2002's April primroses he emerged blinking into sunlight stronger faster and leaner than 'any nineteen year old' and promptly fell down a rabbit hole.

Too late, fitness coach Andy Hurry had the brainwave of introducing yoga at the County Ground to help both suppleness in contortion and concentration of mind. Steffan tried it just the once.

The thoughtless bunny had made its excavation at Millfield and the consequences of Steffan Jones tearing the ligaments in his left ankle warming up for a pre season friendly against Cardiff UCCE would prove to be profound.

However, at the time serious thoughts were hard to muster. Mentions of the offending rabbit come the second week of May continued to cause smirks and the odd unkind giggle. Apple trees blossomed pink. The Blackbird pink-pinked daily and Bumblebees hummed. Down beside the Tone, Yorkshire arrived at the County Ground.

Given the strength of Somerset bowling on paper and having Caddick as the

spearhead – England call-ups permitting – it was unrealistic to expect Jamie Cox to have smelled trouble despite Richard Johnson's knee suddenly deciding to blow up like an ill conceived IED. There was the happy scenario of having Keith Parsons and Simon 'Franco' Francis to call upon if the need arose.

And anyway, 'Bully' Bulbeck had returned to the fold raring to go having been unwrapped from cotton wool. The hope was he could re-establish his rhythm and match fitness after a long lay-off without difficulty. The nasty back injury that sidelined him for most of '01, restricting him to five matches and just four wickets, seemed to have resolved itself. Kevin Shine had enough confidence to say: 'Matt is a potential England bowler. He's half-a-year ahead of schedule, everybody has done a good job to get him back to where he is now.' Great news. Although, perhaps, the video games company *Empire Interactive* had slightly jumped the gun. Their *International Cricket Captain* had turned the blond Somerset left-arm seamer into some sort of modern day all-conquering Richard Hadlee.

Supped early on his homemade scrumpy Phillius broke off from humming *Walzing Matilda* and waggling a broken seat in the River Stand at first sight of both captains at the toss. 'Now we'll see the cut of their cloth,' he said before a polite burp. 'Aussie versus Aussie. May the best swagman outwit and win. I've no doubting that it'll be JC ... and there you go,' Phillius observed, 'he's got first blood.' Jamie having won the toss the Tykes found themselves inserted. Faith had indeed been put in the Somerset bowlers.

Theoretically, Jamie Cox against Darren Lehmann seemed like a pithy encounter between hard nut leaders. Would the taker of the spoils go on to take the Championship at summer's end? It was certainly a possibility given the previous season's form.

But there were just a couple of concerns. 'You know what they say in the Army?' I asked the question rhetorically but seeing Phillius' frown I continued my train of thought. 'A good woman weakens a man. And now to top that Coxy's got a little 'un ... late nights, pre-dawn dark ...' My voice trailed away as I noticed my friend stare unfocused into space as he thoughtfully chewed on his bottom lip. Had I unwittingly touched a nerve?

On the field Coxy's decision to bowl appeared to be vindicated. Within 57 overs Caddy with a 'fifer' and Bully and Franco with a brace apiece nipped out York-shire for 213 in their first innings. But then Chris Silverwood and Matthew Hoggard went to work. Before tea on the first day Somerset were 75 for 6 both Trescothick and Bowler ripped out for 'quackers'. Cox managed a boundary four and nothing more.

Enter the fierce hitting Ian Blackwell – Blackie to some, 'Donkey' to others, or 'Le Donk' just to be perversely multi-cultural. They were names interchangeable as

the mood took it. This potential retriever of lost causes had signed from Derbyshire in 2000 as a spinner who could bat. His batting style, he himself said, aspired to Botham. Against Yorkshire Blackie boy certainly enhanced his own reputation a further notch. By the close of play he was ruddy of face and a bloody centurion.

He only managed to add 8 runs to his tally on the morning of day two before the Tyke's skipper caught him to give Silverwood his third of four hard earned wickets.

As he ruminated on the boundary Silverwood discussed the virtues of the Taunton pitch when he should really have paying attention to goings on in the middle. The 'unresponsive track,' he grumbled, made him mentally and physically tired because he had to 'think the batsmen out more here than anywhere else'. At his age it was too much like hard work. Blackwell had worn him to a frazzle in the Frizzell the previous day by meting out carnage.

Aided by Dutch wading in with 46, Blackie's 13 fours and trio of sixes had put Somerset in the driving seat. At the innings end the home side had a 29 run lead. Second time around the white roses made a better fist of things. Their top order fired before Somerset's attack made the riposte, whipping out the last six Yorkshire wickets for 50 runs to leave a chase of about 260.

Suffering personal drought Coxy failed again to get any worthwhile runs. And despite Burnsy doing similarly it didn't matter a jot. There followed plenty of time for Phillius and I to discuss the pros and cons of fatherhood in between our regular bouts of palm-reddening applause.

After nearly four hours a gentle off-break from Exeter University graduate Richard Dawson shockingly allowed Yorkshire to see the back of Trescothick. He dragged himself back to the Colin Atkinson pavilion visibly cross that he hadn't quite seen Zum over the line. Although, to be fair, with 3 sixes and 18 fours in a score of 134 he hadn't let his team-mates down. Indeed, Peter Bowler was happy enough to let Keith Parsons clobber the small requirement left with seven wickets remaining in the stable. Of these, only Donkey stubbornly bothered to pad up again.

Phillius, content his favoured swagman had triumphed without the need to overly contribute, raised his 'apple juice' flask in salute. However, hailed though it may have been that May, in the four-day game over the length of the season the victory over Yorkshire was unnervingly solitary as by Sod's Law the list of injured pros began to grow. It was as if the three Nornes under Yggdrasil – the Norse tree of Life – had begun to spin the fates with more mischievous intent than a Blackwell chinaman.

To come second in 2001 Somerset had won six matches in the County Champi-

onship and lost just a couple. Come 2002 they lost seven. It could only bode one thing – trouble.

But let it be said in Zum's defence there was a worthy distraction – retaining the C&G Trophy. Summer breezes in July, however, rustled the sick notes. These included Andy Caddick's and Richard Johnson's as a quarter-final against Worcestershire dawned. As it did so John Collis of the *Guardian* lampooned Somerset as 'the living dead'. The County gave whole new meaning to the word 'crockery'.

Desperation called for desperate measures. An 'out of form' Jamie Cox had passed the baton of captaincy to youthful Trescothick. And Paul Jarvis returned from retirement to assist a patched up Steffan Jones who'd been used sparingly in championship cricket to keep him fit for one-day games. Old Father Time though had grown many a grey hair since Paul had blotted his England copybook having chosen to go on the '89/'90 rebel tour of South Africa to pay off his mortgage in one go. He was no longer the 'well-coordinated pace bowler who skiddied the ball through with considerable venom' described by cricket writer Colin Bateman in *If The Cap Fits*.

Toss won, Trescothick asked Worcestershire to bat, and they gratefully accepted. After the early dismissal of Stephen Peters plum ell bee to Steffan, any further contribution to the day from Trescothick abruptly ceased. Jarvis coming on first change to a cheer had Graeme Hick rifle a ball into the offside that cracked into Marcus' thumb. A capacity crowd felt the pain. The Somerset skipper left the field immediately, his left hand as limp as a flaccid kipper. Meanwhile, Jarvis disappeared for 25 in two overs and, to all intents and purposes, wasn't seen again either.

Hick and Solanki toyed sadistically with depleted Zum, adding 81 in 11 overs. Looking like being 350 against 10 dispirited men, Cox, suddenly finding himself captain again, was having none of it. Showing a radar vision in the field and an imagination that Trescothick was yet to learn he placed his faith in Keith Parsons to rewrite the script and nab the match.

Keith obliged, playing at a level higher than the performance that had earned him Man of the Match in the previous season's final. He had reined back the Pears with ten cheap overs and two wickets, including demolishing the stumps the scourge Hick; taken two outrageously good catches and ended Worcester's innings with a direct-hit to run out Aussie Matt Mason.

Having 'stars' is wonderful, everyone loves to see them, but having someone who can apply skills within a game situation is far more important. Keith Parsons got more than 100 first-class wickets by moving the ball both ways and teasing people out. In *The Flame Still Burns*, Stephen Chalke's biography of Tom Cartright, here

was the guru who the 'Demon of Frome' Colin Dredge recognized as the ultimate bowler. Proud Tom, loyal to the values of his working-class upbringing, holds firmly to a vision of cricket as a people's game, rooted in communities and upholding high standards of craft skill and of behaviour. Not for him a game in thrall to accountants and television moguls. And likewise with Keith locally embedded in Taunton St Andrews.

Due largely to his efforts, Worcester's 271, bowled out with an over to spare, was considerably less than they had threatened.

However, Peter Bowler and Cox still needed to build a goodly foundation, and to their chagrin they both fell snicking expansive drives. Burnsy and the redoubtable Parsons began the repair work with 51 runs, but the crowd was fidgety knowing Zum vulnerability without Trescothick. Yes, he'd returned to the ground but could hardly win a match with droopy flipper.

Donkey came and went having raised hopes but the glory of a match-winning partnership was left to Parsons and Rob Turner, crab-like of stance but a limpet at the crease. Orv lingered a mere 100 balls for a phenomenal 121 constructed from 15 fours and a mighty six. Both he and Rob both demised, but in evening heat Keith Dutch and Bully Bulbeck belted Somerset to a home semi-final with Kent. And it proved to be an occasion that would live long in the memory.

I hadn't witnessed a game like it since '78 when, in the semi-final of the Gillette Cup, Somerset defeated Essex by virtue of losing fewer wickets. This was thanks to a Viv Richards ton, the Demon of Frome just about holding his nerve when bowling the last over with whole of his enormous family behind his arm, and famously a last ball run out contrived between a rubber legged Brian Rose and wicky Derek Somerset Taylor. I can still hear the BBC commentary in my head now: 'Last ball of the match. Three runs required. The last pair together. If Colin Dredge bowls another no ball they'll hang him here...' Then it was harum-scarum mayhem.

The 2002 semi-final was equally wonderful and perhaps the finest limited overs county game of the noughties. On the 1st of August Bulbeck was awarded his county cap and well before the start of play the early birds had gathered. In anticipation of a long day stout carrier bags were stuffed with foodie sustenance, newspapers, Suduku puzzlers and thumbed bestsellers. A lady with a crochet needle and balls of wool stood making blanket squares. Swans gliding about in the Tone waters at the back of the Sir Ian Botham Stand were joined by flotillas of ducks and a cormorant that sat, it's drying wings outstretched. Overhead a squadron of gulls circled. All were hopeful of morsels from the multitude of us keen supporters queuing up on the river walk waiting to squeeze ourselves into the best vantage points. As the feathered scavengers gulped and squabbled over lean pickings one could only hope Kent's bowlers would be more obliging with their offerings.

It transpired that they were. Zum, however, were equally profligate.

At my first mention of the thrash to Keith Parsons he gave a smile as broad as his bat. 'It was an incredible game,' he said. 'Batting first we got what in those days was a huge score. It was obviously a very, very good wicket as they often were in those days but we thought we'd got plenty. Everyone who went in scored as soon as they went out there.'

Having been put in Somerset negotiated the morning moisture and their tally was, indeed, impressive. 344 for 5 from their 50 overs, thanks to some aggressive batting later on in the innings, which saw 194 runs scored from the last 20 overs.

Veteran Peter Bowler survived an early chance when he was dropped in the second over, but then took the score onto 59 before he lost Captain Cox for 31. Always strong on the leg-side Peter also cut and drove well behind square. He looked set for a century before he was bowled by a dipping in-swinger from the 'Brum' born Aussie Andrew Symonds. His 70 though had helped set things up abetted by Mike Burns, who at 33 and six years Peter's junior, batted even better. He accelerated after a slow start, hitting six fours and a straight six that bonked a hapless TV cameraman on the noggin. After an exemplary 72 he departed going for another gurt tonk, caught at cover by the hop county's captain and aspiring politician Matthew Fleming.

In a game cluttered with fantastic displays of clean hitting, Blackwell stood out. His knock was full of dashing drives and massive heaves, with the odd elegant touch thrown in. After reaching 50 from 32 balls, he launched a six straight down the ground. A butter-fingered Fleming at long-on dropped him on 83, only for Symonds to be less careless at long-off 3 runs later.

Keith, Rob Turner and Dutch all weighed in, with the latter finding the middle of the bat at the death. And the 20 runs hit off the last over would prove themselves to be vital.

'Everyone was buzzing at halfway thinking here we go we're going to be at Lord's again,' said Keith. 'And then all of a sudden we just couldn't defend anything. 'Kent had a flying start. Fleming came out and flayed it everywhere. He and Rob Key had the fifty up in the ninth over. I was introduced into the attack for the fourteenth over and off the fourth ball Key chopped the ball onto his stumps.' Kent were 105 for 1.

In the next over Fleming chased a ball from Steffan and was caught by Rob Turner, and in Keith's following over he trapped James Hockley ell bee.

In the space of three overs 100 for nowt had become to 122 for 3, and Zum hopes lifted on a roller-coaster ride. Kent had added a further 68 before Donkey tempted

Symonds into top edging an injudicious sweep.

'Coxy took a good catch running in from behind Rob.' Keith recalled. 'And it got to the stage when the run rate was creeping up and we were sort of just hanging in there but they were still scoring at just under the rate. It was ticking up a little bit but the game getting closer and closer.'

Going into the final twenty overs Kent needed 130 to win and seemed to be chugging easily towards their target until, first ball of the 38th over, the Parsons golden arm accounted for both David Fulton, who spooned a long-hop down the throat of deep mid-wicket, and Matthew Walker. 262 for 6. Still, Kent edged towards their target. Kent keeper Paul Nixon and Mark Ealham took the score to within 9 runs and were bossing the game having already put on 74 for the seventh wicket

What happened next was extraordinary. I had glimpsed Richard Johnson disappear from the field but, like everybody else around me in the River Stand, had no idea where he had offed as we chorused 'C'mon Blackie, give us a wave, give us wave' at Donkey patrolling the boundary beneath us. The roar he received upon raising his hand coincided with the appearance on the field of twelfth man Simon Francis.

Keith explained all with a snigger. Jono went off to get the ball that had been hit over the stands by Matt Walker. Climbing back over the fence he got hamstring cramp and had to go off the field through injury.

With the game all but won the Kent wheels came off. Steffan clearly remembered what happened. 'We were looking at the scoreboard and thought this is getting a bit tight here. There must have been 5 overs left and Bully, back from injury, was bowling beautifully the other end. Then I bowled to 'Nicko' – Paul Nixon – and he didn't take a single. He went 'oh, no no no,' and we all picked up on it.

'And we thought hang on here he's being very lackadaisical. They're taking this for granted.'

Suddenly feeling the pressure Nixon backed-up too far and was run-out by an alert Dutch prowling at midwicket. James Golding followed the Kent 'keeper back to the pavilion almost immediately. The run out Francis contrived was amazing to behold. All in one movement he dived across picked up the ball and hurled it as he was tumbling over. When David Masters walked to the wicket Kent required just 7 runs for victory from 8 balls. The penultimate over went for just two runs when, off its last ball, Bulbeck disarrayed Masters' stumps.

All this left a rather bewildered Ealham needing six from the final over with the last man Martin Saggers at the other end. The Welsh bison was given the onerous job of bowling it in a cauldron of noise. Putting rabbit hole niggles to the back of

his mind this was what he had trained for. The mental state of the good folk of Somerset rested on his shoulders. In he charged, puce in the face with effort for the first delivery. In the stands young and the not quite so closed their eyes or covered them with their hands. Ealham swung to midwicket. Dutch took an exemplary tumbling catch.

Cue pure unadulterated tumult. The River Stand throbbed. The lady with the crochet had created barely enough to blanket a robust Blackbird and was shriek-ing as if on a hen night in Weston-super-Mare with Cox and Co. her Chippen-dales. Possibly all too much for the cormorant, it arrowed away overhead undoubtedly bound for the quieter gatherings of the Brewhouse Theatre or indeed the safer waters that lay far beyond.

'And as it happened,' Steffan confessed to me, 'it wasn't a great ball to Ealham. But I was always told it was better to bowl a full toss than a drag down half volley. So it was a low full toss and he just picked it up to Duchy. And I remember being carried off the field.

'What a game of cricket that was!' Never have truer words been uttered.

Somerset had snatched a 5 run victory from what had looked like a certain defeat just a few minutes earlier. Kent lost their last four wickets for three runs.

'You look back at Simon Francis,' Keith reflected, 'and that was a major, major influence on that game. His sprawling effort got the danger man out and we sneaked over the line.

'It was a regular joke about Jono getting damaged regularly. To think that him getting injured climbing over a fence, enabling us to get through to the final was hilarious. Jono surely wouldn't have performed the run out that Franco did.'

Somerset and Kent had shared nearly 700 runs as a full house sang, drank and roared through a warm, sunny day. Chasing Somerset's massive 344 for 5, Kent were bowled out for 339.

As I joined the crowds thronging onto the pitch Blackwell was named as a very popular Man of the Match for being the fulcrum of the Somerset innings and taking the pace off the ball when the Kent batsmen were running amok. Those around me started to chat animatedly about the trip to Lord's at August's end and the chances of Trescothick being fit.

After the game a relieved Kevin Shine commented: 'I've just spent the last fifty overs wearing out the carpet in the dressing room. We have to be confident of retaining the trophy. That win really does show the character that we have in our team.

Chief Executive Peter Anderson felt compelled to add: 'I've seen most things in the game of cricket but never seen anything quite like that.'

In the *Guardian* Paul Weaver was tongue in cheek. 'As a prospective Conservative Party candidate Matthew Fleming, the captain of Kent, appeared to have made the shrewd decision to familiarise himself with landslide defeats.'

After the potential cardiac arrests of the semi-final the Lord's final versus Yorkshire was an anticlimax between two sides finding themselves nestled at the bottom of the County Championship Division 1. For both, relegation had become a certainty, their table placing a total reversal of the previous season's fortunes.

I asked Steffan how he could explain what, at first glance, appeared to be a fiasco.

Seeing him become absorbed in thought, I prompted: 'Was it the yoga?'
He shrugged, and several moments passed before he answered.

'What we had in 2001 was great team spirit,' he sighed reflectively. 'Richard Johnson and I loved bowling in tandem with one other. We became good friends. We worked as a partnership. A lot of the games I'd take top three but he would clean up the tail, or the other way round.

'Then I was injured. And Jono was injured. That's a hundred-and-twenty wickets there 'cos we took that number between us the year before. I think I got a hundred in all cricket or maybe it was ninety-nine.' A slight smile played at the corner of his mouth but it was gone in a jiffy. 'So you take those out …

'You know what? I think that was it. A hundred-and-twenty wickets is a lot from two bowlers not really available to play in 2002. The ligament damage caused from falling down that rabbit hole meant I had to battle through discomfort all season. I kept pulling my hamstring 'cos I was carrying my left leg. Jono's knee kept blowing and he, too, kept pulling his hamstring.

'In 2000 and 2001 I think I bowled a thousand Championship overs and took a hundred-and ten wickets. That was a lot of overs. And if you take so many wickets out of a side you're going to struggle. And the bowlers who came in obviously couldn't take them.' I cottoned on Steffan wasn't blowing his own trumpet. He was merely being honest.

His thoughts on the final were equally as erudite.

It mattered not a fig that, his thumb mended, Trescothick was back in the side. Yorkshire chased down Somerset's total, limited by lacklustre wafts, playing across the line and insipid drives, to a modest 256 for 8 to win by six wickets with a couple of overs in hand, and ended an era. The match was the last limited over

occasion where the players wore whites. The new-fanglement of coloured pyjamas was on its way in.

Equally of note, the game had the pleasure of a superlative umpire. That's to say John Holder came from Superlative in the West Indies. The other ump, George 'Razor' Sharp, much to Steffan's evident distress, couldn't lay claim to a heritage anywhere near as consummate.

In an innings that was perfunctory rather than dazzling Man of the Match Chelsea's Matthew Elliott – that's Chelsea in the state of Victoria – hit 100 in 110 balls and finished on 128 not out to ensure Somerset did not retain the trophy in a on-sided Lord's final.

Steffan remains scathing towards his team-mates' lassitude. I gave one hundred per cent every game. That game I knew I was carrying my leg but ran in and gave it absolutely everything. As I came off at end of play, Mark Garraway was the coach then said: "do you know what? If every county had someone who gave as much as you the game would be in a better position."

'I gave everything. I was exhausted. And I remember I got Michael Vaughan out ell bee and next ball McGrath – well, he should have been out ell bee, too. That would have won us the game. Definitely would 'cos he went on to get runs. But George gave him not out.'

A case of a Hartlepool Razor cutting off Zum hope, I thought.

Self-righteous indignation welled in Steffan. 'A day or so later up in Durham for a National League game we had videos and we asked the umpires Mark Benson, and Merv Kitchen to have a look. And Merv said: 'Don't tell me that's not out.' It was a shocking decision. I still know George now.' More than that Steffan was reticent to say.

But looking back at Tykes victory Keith Parsons didn't seem too upset. 'By beating Kent,' he said, 'Somerset had already had their final'.

In the Championship, Somerset and Yorkshire continued their rivalry as if tied at the hip. It was be neck and neck as to which came bottom. Both sides had finished level on points.

Having a quarter point stripped from them for a slow over-rate in match against Leicestershire on 12th September should have given Somerset the dubious wreath. However, elsewhere Yorkshire had transgressed further ensuring bottom berth was theirs.

Relegation was an ignominy Jamie Cox found hard to stomach. Although willing

to stay at the club as a batter the captaincy was something he didn't want more. And with things not right, bouncy, jovial Mike Burns, who as it transpired was the season's top run scorer, accepted a poisoned chalice that other contenders shied away from.

'Burnsy's decision changed him,' commented the Welsh bison. True. Almost as much as a bunny-hopper had Steffan.

Chief executive Peter Anderson was sufficiently baffled by the team's miserable form to send a letter of apology to each member, many of whom were equally bamboozled if not a tad resentful. 'Too many of our performances,' Peter wrote, 'seemed to lack enthusiasm, urgency, and the requisite application expected of professional players.' Every coach and player within the club was interviewed and players were left smarting by the very public rebuke. The message was clear. 'You got us down; now blinking well get us back up.'

SEVEN

Bish, Bosh and Burns Unit

*'Talents are best nurtured in solitude, but character
is best formed in the stormy billows of the world.'*
Johann Wolfgang von Goethe (German writer, 1749-1832).

Puffing away, sweat oozing from his pores, that lover of hot Indian curry, chirpy former Somerset skipper Mike Burns was using his time well in the County Ground's gym. I wouldn't say he was a typical tough Northerner. He had spent long enough down the West Country not to be. The evergreen fitness fanatic was stretching his legs upon the treadmill and other similarly knackering apparatus in preparation for his opening season as an umpire on the reserve list for the first-class circuit. A Merv Kitchen in the making, perhaps.

It seemed an age ago since the curmudgeons in the *Bearin' Up* spoke scathingly on two counts at the beginning of the 2003 season. By hoping to put bums on seats, wee-willy-winkies in pyjamas befitting Primark would be battling it out in new-fangled twenty over bouts of hit and giggle at the County Ground. And Zum, bother it, was to be led by an ex-welder with a comic streak.

Mike Burns, though, whose natural game, on paper, had been ideal for the fledgling format, proved less and less a Billy Connelly as his tenure wore on.
'Worse thing Burnsy did was take the captaincy,' Steffan Jones remarked. 'I know it's a tough thing to say "no" to captaining Somerset, but Mike was like I was – heart and soul of the dressing room, lots of banter, we bounced off each other. But as soon as he got the captaincy the fun time was over. Overwhelmed by seriousness, he lost his sparkle.'

However, Burnsy may not have been the world-beater of an Ian Botham or Keiron Pollard, but he was the very example of making the best of what he had, driven by his passion for the game. No, he didn't perform particularly well during his captaincy, but due to him being so passionate about Somerset County Cricket Club he should be forgiven. Like many 'furriners', the Cumbrian educated at Walney Comprehensive had found himself sucked in by the County's magnetism. Yet, he has never forgotten where he came from, the antithesis of lads going through the system even now that were picked up very early at public school; those having a lot of contacts and a privileged lifestyle.

'Ah, the Burns Unit.' Phillius spoke reflectively stood amongst the shavings as he rasped smooth the wooden prow of his latest boat commission. 'In its first year it was notable only, I think, for being injury prone, and for Nixon McLean and The Gilder.'

Well, that was succinct, I had thought to myself. Smiley, gap-toothed Nixon had been one of the new wave of West Indian fast bowlers. His middle names Alexei McNamara, however, were more impressive than his Test average: 42.56. I could only wonder at the aspirations Nixon's parents had for him and his siblings when christened in Stubbs church perched atop a little rocky, windblown, sea battered promontory in St Vincent.

With hopes seemingly not lying in cricket, Somerset's new signing arrived, via KwaZulu-Natal, saddled with the names of an American president (Richard Nixon), a Russian prime minister (Alexei Kosygin) and an American defence secretary (Robert McNamara). His brothers are called Reagan and Kissinger, and his sister got lumbered with Golda, after Golda Meir the fourth Prime Minister of Israel.

As a number 11, however, Nixon showed himself to be the accomplished king of the jackrabbits. Missed by Derbyshire off the first ball he faced in Somerset's final home championship match of the summer he knuckled down to partner Ian Blackwell to the Cidermen's highest last-wicket partnership and, as it transpired, a rare win to elevate the county to 7th in the second division.

'Blackie', or 'Donkey' depending on one's predilection, played the innings of his life with a breathtaking 247 in 156 balls on the day he was picked for England's one-day squad for Bangladesh and Sri Lanka. Of his 11 sixes, four were lost in the adjoining graveyard, and he blasted 27 more deliveries to the boundary in what the *Telegraph* described as 'an extraordinary display of brute force, immaculate timing and well-judged placement'. Together the pair put on 163 in an hour, taking them past 400. The feat had looked improbable at 75 for six, following a morning of disasters, including James Hildreth on debut having his poles pranged by Dominic Cork. And it was all brought on by Captain Burnsy's puzzling decision to bat first under cloudy skies.

Blackwell's first 50 came in 62 balls, then he hit a towering six to reach 1,000 first-class runs for the first time in his career. He hit another straight six to bring up the century in 93 balls, and grinning all the way after he heard the news of his England selection, moved into top gear by scoring his next 100 in a whirlwind 41 deliveries.

Upon Nixon finally falling ell bee to Mohammad Ali, Blackie, unbeaten, lapped up the standing ovation.

That support-act apart, Nixon's other claim to fame was his 'discovery' of the enigma that remains the Zimbabwean Gary Gilder. Whatever Nixon might seen in the garden province home of the Zulu nation didn't translate to Taunton pitches. Somerset certainly gambled on the club cricketer whose attempts at South African first class cricket in 01/02 returned one wicket at an average of 88.00. There were no stats visible for 02/03. To sign the Zimbabwean upon the Windward Islander's tip-off smacked either of desperation or a cunning ploy to ease the strain on the afflicted bowling department.

As it was, Gilder made his Somerset debut on 21st July, the day the County Ground's Sir Vivian Richards gates were inaugurated. The opposition was a charitable pub side of some note – the Lashings 'dream team' of world cricket stars. Sherwin Campbell and Ritchie Richardson licked their lips and proceeded to clatter our unfortunate Gary to all parts.

He played his third and last match in mid August at Taunton against Northants. The visitors amassed 681 for 5 declared after 169 overs during which Mike Hussey clouted 331 and Sales and Bailey chipped in with a hundred apiece. McLean, Jones, Blackwell, Laraman, Burns, Edwards, Webley, and Cox all turned their arm over. But not Gary. He gave new meaning to the phrase 'strike bowler' partaking in a game that, for him, must have seemed more black ball than red.

Nudging Nixon up to number 10, he snicked his way to 7 not out in Somerset's first innings, the lowest score on the card, including extras, and was never called upon by Captain Burns to bowl a single ball throughout the whole of Northants long sole effort. Was he too much of a risk? Heavens above, a matter of days earlier he'd bagged a brace in the National League, including having enticed Sales to snick to the gauntleted Gazzard.

But at the County Ground, and with Gazzard occupying his prescribed place behind the stumps excused a bowl, only top of the order Matt Wood remained snubbed a go with an increasingly battered cherry.

While Gary vegetated on the boundary in front of the sparsely populated River Stand I distracted him from intently nibbling his nails by asking him to sign my son's signature bat. And this is where he indelibly remains, just under the Great

Wall of India, Rahul Dravid.

I had to acknowledge that 2003 proved the undoing of not just The Gilder but of other Somerset hopefuls, too.

South African Jamie Bryant came and went. Suffering from a lack of confidence and homesickness throughout his season stay, he banished those demons for three sessions. His 160 contributed significantly to Zum's massive 701 for 9 in a dull, run drenched draw against Hampshire.

And on the morning 30th July, as Zum prepared themselves at the Riverside to play Durham, the *Daily Echo* trumpeted: 'Bournemouth left-hander Tom Webley to his County Championship debut for Somerset – against the fastest bowler in the world!!!'

The newspaper failed to mention the bowler concerned had played for Somerset, albeit the once, and reportedly could start a fight in an empty room. The Rawalpindi Express, Shoaib Akhtar, had donned whites for Somerset versus Ricky Ponting's Australia in 2001. Shoaib was joined in the Somerset eleven by Aamir Sohail. The latter played a big part in Pakistan's World Cup triumph in 1992, and famously told Ian Botham that he might want to send his mother-in-law in to bat after Botham was controversially given out for 0 in the final.

'We introduced the two Pakistan players to add interest to the fixture,' said chief executive Peter Anderson.

Against Durham, Somerset lost by 316 runs. Zum capitulated to 56 all out in their second innings. Rawalpindi Expressed, Cambridge Blue Tom Webley got a golden duck. Some baptism of fire.

Being a bits and pieces player – wicketkeeper, batter and bowler – Captain Burnsy could empathize with what individual members of his team were going through because he'd been there himself. 'Look,' he would say, 'come on, I know this is going to be tough so do it with a smile on your face and hopefully we'll get through it.' That might or might not have helped have Tom or, indeed, the rest of the younger players.

* * *

Wailing seagulls circled. Spectres rather than spectators above the County Ground they seemed a tad confused – a result maybe of their favourite buffet restaurant getting a rebrand from 'Council Tip' to 'Civic Amenity Site' or maybe from the many supporters saying that it was the cricket on view in early season 2004 that had been underwhelming rubbish.

Brian Rose had returned to the County Ground, this time bearing the title Director of Cricket. And in mid May Durham arrived to make a general nuisance of themselves. The northerners may have won by a single wicket largely due to Jamaica's Gareth Breese clobbering 165 not out, but for the home support the honours had to go to James Hildreth for his maiden championship century.

To quote Viv Richards: 'Batsmen can sometimes be intimidated by a guy from how far he runs up. But you just put that at the back of your mind and bat with what you have.' Against the Rawlpindi Express Hildy, batting with Jamie Cox, followed the advice.

On the big stage Shoaib was out to intimidate the fledgling barely out of Millfield, the great nursery of the game whose motto *Molire Molendo* roughly translates as 'drive forward by grinding'. The Pakastani quick steamed in from the Old Pavilion sightscreen every time Hildy faced and when Coxy was on strike he just trotted in from a couple of yards. Coxy would take a single and Shoaib would pelt in again. It was the making of Hildreth who hit a baker's dozen of fours and pair of sixes before Shoaib eventually got him.

In that season's Twenty20 Somerset's poor all round form cricket led to other teams taking the mickey. And in one of the first games of its kind on telly the ribaldry around Somerset calling themselves the Sabres reached a wide audience. During floodlight pre-match banter and in the glare of Sky TV cameras Gloucestershire's skipper Mark Alleyne was asked about Zum's chances. Earning his nickname 'Boo Boo' mostly aptly he had scoffed: 'They're only the Scabbers.'

His quip relayed live to the crowd via Zum's loudspeaker system roused many a boo and grumble of local self-righteous indignation, although by the game's end Mark's cheeky confidence had found basis. The failing Burns Unit got bludgeoned, the Shire winning by whopping margin of 8 wickets.

But, oh how things were set to change. And Phillius wasn't the only one who would be delighted.

EIGHT

Hog, Fog, Puddles and Punter

'We make a living by what we get, but we make a life by what we give.'
Winston Churchill.

On the high reaches of Exmoor, tangles of gnarled and twisted hobbit pines hide an ancient stone row the length of several cricket pitches put nose to tail. This place was once the haunt of the holy man Saint Beuno who despite believing in angels in white probably never hallucinated about the summer game. And definitely not coloured pyjamas. Hereabouts bats tend to be pipistrelles, leather is made into saddles and 'furriners' tend to become bored.

Unsurprisingly, it was a newsworthy event when a whole bundle of sporty outsiders congregated one winter's Sunday evening at the *Culbone* gastropub at the suggestion of Minehead Cricket Club. Thoughts of vespers probably never entered a single head as everyone stuffed themselves silly and roared at anecdotes from a lauded duo. One who thrived on hearty renditions of *'Sweet Chariot'* and *Jerusalem* and, and the other with soft spots for *The Blackbird* and Kuala Lumpur.

Warmed nicely by ribald anecdotes from the former England & British Lions rugby star Mark Regan MBE Arul Suppiah's Benefit Year was under way. Thirteen years a Zum player, Arul was one of a handful to have witnessed all the 21st century had thrown at the cricket mad county.

And if any cricketer granted a benefit needed a hook to help promote himself then by golly '6 for 5' was a grand one. Without doubt more eye-catching than his 3 for 46 against West Indies A on his first team debut in July 2002 that remain his

best first-class bowling, the figures were astonishing and a world-record return – but only if the amateurs were discounted.

Regrettably there wasn't much in the way of record logging as Huish & Langport's Dominic Shillabeer bagged seven Barrington wickets for two runs in 2012. In a message on the club's website, Dominic expressed his personal surprise: 'Well, Well, Well!!! What to say!'

The Somerset folk squeezed into that isolated pub had said nowt. Biased, they only wished to be reminded of how Arul's haul came about.

During a rain affected T20 game on 5th July 2011 in Cardiff, Arul's figures bettered Sohail Tanvir's six for 14 for Rajasthan against Chennai in Jaipur in May 2008, and came from 3.4 overs. The Welsh county were dismissed for just 98 as Arul's left-arm spin ripped through their batting. Allenby, Cooke, Harris, Croft and Simon and Alex Jones constituted 'Ruley's' procession of Dragons. Murali Kartik and Max Waller shared the remaining wickets between themselves and Somerset were 'Pollarded' to victory with 21 balls to spare.

Now Ruley was due for an appointment at the County Ground, Keith Parson told me. Somerset County Sports were having their pre-season sale and the benefit boy would be signing copies of his brochure.

'To have a benefit year is an honour,' said Keith.

I still remember his in 2004. Keith had a Somerset versus Durham totesport League Division 2 game chosen as his benefit match. The northerners' pitched up at the end of June bringing inclement weather with them. Stumpy the Zum mascot could have done with a brolly as wandered the boundary edge waggling a bucket to entice much coinage while imploring fivers, tenners and twenties in notes. Fifties were pushing it for a not very scary, tall, furry maroon wyvern.

The game itself was squib of the dampest kind. Injured, Keith couldn't play although his kid brother Mike did, and Durham, aided by brotherly Pratt's Alan and Gary, won on Duckworth/Lewis.

However, Keith had other opportunities to generate some cash for himself. I heard of one that was imminent upon wandering into Triscombe's *Blue Ball Inn*, run by a couple from London's Park Lane who were 'slumming it' charging Somerset prices. The barman, thick accented with the brogue of Zum, played for Stogumber. They, he proudly announced, pausing halfway in pulling my pint, were to play Somerset.

Penelope Lively's Gothic novel *The Wild Hunt of Hagworthy* mentions Stogumber as 'magical, infinitely familiar', but it palpably makes no reference to boys in

fields rummaging for six hit cricket balls. On the match day not only was the hog roast smoking.

Ducking and diving, Marcus Trescothick ambled the boundary rope, chatting to all-and-sundry who were hanging off every word. It prompted a sun-hatted pensioner lady sat in a picnic chair and sipping chilled Chablis from an ice bucket to turn to women of similar years next to her. 'What a very, very nice man. Who the devil is he?' Keith instantly gave up all hope of recognition.

What were the chances of Ricky 'Punter' Ponting knowing him by sight on the drizzly day he arrived? Keith must have been cagey about that to start with. However, when the non-evident sun finally slipped below the yardarm a day later he had become more than optimistic.

'Ricky was pure quality from the minute he came,' said humble Keith, still awestruck after so many years. Without a shadow of doubt the Aussie phenomenon had been eagerly awaited to bolster Somerset's top order. The date of his arrival had been tattooed inside chief executive Peter Anderson's eyelids: July 15. Forty-eighty beforehand Zum lost to Nottinghamshire after having batted with all the nous of dim-witted lemmings. 'He'll have to bat one, two, three, four and five,' said the Peter, not entirely whimsically. So needy were Zum of his services that Punter barely had time to draw breath.

'A few hours from touching down at London Heathrow on that Thursday July morning he was changed and playing a Twenty20 against Northants. He ran Hildy out for nought.' Keith chuckled.

'After the game I was walking around the dressing room trying to find eleven lads to come along to my benefit game the following night at Taunton Deane's little ground behind Vivary Park.

'Ricky pipes up: "what's going on, Pars?"

"Oh, I've got a benefit game tomorrow night."

"Well, I'll play."

I was gobsmacked. "You sure?" I said.

"Yer, yer, I'm here to play cricket. I'll come a play."

"It's only a club game, you won't have to do anything, just come along if you like."

"No mate, no mate, I'll come and play. I've got me kit."

I thought, oh fantastic. He was living in the flats over in the Octagon near the ground so I said I'd pick you up.

"That'd be great." He was very enthusiastic.

I remained a bit hedgy. "We'll see tomorrow whether you wanna play or not. It really is up to you. If you just show your face that'd be great."

So it's absolutely hammering it down all afternoon. So I go and pick him up at 5 o'clock and he goes and says: "what's going on? We won't play will we?"

"No," I replied, "but you know what club cricketers are like. As soon as it stops we'll push the covers off and have a game, if that's alright." And I added: 'don't worry. Don't risk getting injured or anything silly." I was thinking, no way can we get Ricky Ponting skidding about on a wet field.

"Okay," he said. And still he comes dragging his big bag bringing all his kit expecting to play.

The rain was pouring down as we both rocked up at the Deane. Then, within an hour, there was this sheet of white cloud coming over. "Right," said someone, "let's get these covers off and let's get going.' So we did start, despite the grass being soaking wet and drizzle still falling.

"Never mind, Rick," I said. "Don't worry about it anymore."

And all he said was: "C'mon, where do you want me to bat?"

So I had Marcus opening and Ricky batting 3 for me in a benefit game at Taunton Deane. And I also had Caddick, McLean and Johnson. It was the right sort side that we couldn't get out in first-class games most of the time. Ricky went out and batted, and I think he got 30 odd before chipping an Aussie who was playing for them in the air to give someone else a go. Afterwards he stayed behind and had a chat, mixing with the local boys and the local club. Those were real special moments for everyone. What a fantastic guy! And it was a good thing for me, too. I wondered to myself whether Ruley might get a similar accommodating gesture from Alviro Peterson. Time would tell.

In Keith's mind the way Punter batted was pure quality. It was an opinion shared by others. Sir Viv Richards had commented: 'Ricky always made the crease his house. Because of (his) brashness he's an in-your-face sort of guy. Shows no fear. Ricky, to me, certainly did that.' And the Pollock story emphasized it, and it was nowt to do with leaky boat, Bristol Channel sea-fishing.

Shaun Pollock had beaten past the outside edge of Punter's Test match bat with

a couple of deliveries. As a follow up the South African sniped: 'It's red, round and weighs about five ounces.' The next ball crashed into the pickets and Punter riposted: 'You know what it looks like, now go find it.'

A week after the small affair of the Deane game Punter was breathing the sea air of Scarborough. He might have arrived too late in the season to transform Zum from winless also-rans into promotion candidates, but a Rolls-Royce of a pre-lunch century gave majestic definition to his championship debut.

16 not out overnight, and bar a couple of awkward moments against Steve Kirby on the third day's opening over, Ponting's mastery was complete. Compact in defence, he cover drove exquisitely and reached his hundred in the grand manner, advancing on off-spinner Richard Dawson to launch an effortless six over wide long-on and become the first Somerset player on championship debut to make a century since Andy Hayhurst in 1990.

'I remember one innings he played at Durham in a day/night game,' said Keith, retrieving another Punter gem from his personal memory bank. 'There was a really thick mist coming across the Riverside and it was like batting in a dirty old nightclub in the old days when nightclubs were smoky. You could hardly see the scoreboard across the other side of the ground. And he got 70 or 80 not out. It was pure quality from a fantastic player.

As an aside, against Yorkshire at Taunton that September Jamie Cox played his last game for Somerset in any form of cricket. In a rain affected match he didn't even get a bat.

NINE

Wonders of Biff

'To have news value is to have a tin can tied to one's tail.'

T. E. Lawrence.

Wildlife has a sixth sense about cats. When the phone rang that morning there was no rich, sweet whistling from the garden Blackbird. Instead, the bird's persistent 'pink, pink' spread tweets of alarm. Had the bundle of feathers decided Middlesex Panthers were a bigger risk to Zum's cricket fortunes than sanguine cider drinkers had previously thought? Or had the bird got the wrong end of the stick upon hearing about local English Lions Hildreth and Buttler? The answer was pure conjecture, until I felt the unease in the pit of my tummy as my brain deciphered deep voiced Afrikaans.

'Hey, HWEE-uh MOR-uh, Chaz! Hoo Hahn dit?' It was my biltong chewing cousin Chris on the other end of the line wishing me good morning and asking after my health.

'Chris! Huut DON-key.' My reply wasn't an intended reference to Ian Blackwell's nickname. I merely said I was fine. 'For what do I owe the pleasure?' I asked before adding 'Are you pissed?' I'm a firm believer in the adage: if you have a story to tell wait until you're drunk and it'll sound twice as good.

Chris snorted his indignation at the slight. There had indeed been a problem with a lion – a South African born one. Happily, it wasn't Hobnob Kieswetter. Having sworn his allegiance to both Zum and England, he tended to be reasonably tame unless faced with a hard red or white ball directed his way. The lion described by Chris was of the wild furry sort and had found its way into his White River

country club restaurant kitchen causing apoplexy in the chefs preparing meat.

For Chris, born a smote of leather away from Kruger National Park, it had been the excuse he needed. He'd counted the grey hairs at his temples, sucked in his paunch and plotted a visit to Blighty where my spare room was at the forefront of his planning. Zum had been the adopted home of his childhood hero, the exceptional batsman turned batting coach Jimmy Cook. And if it was good enough for Jimmy it had occurred to Chris that it was a more than an attractive sanctuary.

'Problem? Of course there's no problem. The day after tomorrow?' I winced, avoiding my wife's sudden glare and growl. 'What? ... No, it's a bad line.... You want a gander at the Proteus? ... And their second eleven? ... Oh, Somerset ... Ha ha, very funny.'

Yet there was a ring of truth about the quip. There was an evident South African umbilical amongst Trescothick's band of cricketing sweat gatherers. In addition to Hobnob and just off the top of my head there was The Great Alfonso, Meschede the Tendulkar Getter, and Compo Dog, not to mention Big Vern Philander, Jean Genie Levi, and Bert Morkel.

And best of all Biff, the inspirational mountain from Johannesburg Graeme Smith, would be making his return to the county he skippered in 2005 to a wonderful win over Australia and, or course, to Oval silverware. One doesn't like to mention finishing 8th out of nine in Division 2 of the Championship. Although, that said, the 10-1 odds of winning it given at beginning of the season had been fair. Dismissing teams twice on the flat Taunton pitch was the excuse.

'It'll be good to see Jimmy's protégé back in the stomping ground,' said Chris. 'But is it safe?'

'Whatcha mean?'

'Your pre-season guns and stuff. Sounds like you're getting the problems we've got in Jo'burg.'

'What?'

'Don't tell you know nothing about the shooting at Somerset. At the cricket club itself. Plenty of people about at the time. There've been detectives, forensics, the works.'

'Total rubbish.'

'Just saying.'

'Anyway, gotta go. Look forward to seeing you. Have a safe flight. Give us a call a call on your arrival,' I said, prompting wifely wide-eyed incredulity.

'Dankie, bru,' Chris enthused.

'But they'll be no pub quizzes…' I blurted just as we were cut off. The last time he was over had been in June '05, and to be honest he'd made me look a complete plonker while on his part he exhibited a worrying tendency to be right.

'Jimmy Sinclair hit the longest six ball in the history of cricket. Where's he buried?' the lugubrious question master had asked in a close run contest. Our team's 'reliables' began to discuss amongst themselves. Chris, invited by me to be a team guest, lent over and whispered in my ear what I took to be 'Yeovil'.

"You sure?' I frowned, turning to look him in the eye. 'It's news to me.'

'Never surer,' Chris affirmed before sitting back with a smug grin on his face.

'When did he tonk it?' I said sotto voce.

"Bout the Boer War, I guess,' he murmured under his breath. 'When our cricket fields were buffalo grass and wickets were matting. Victorian times to you.'

'Give me an answer or I'll pass it over' coaxed the question master.

'Somerset,' I blurted. Cue consternation from the 'reliables' and a splutter from my cousin.

'That's the wrong answer. Away team, any idea?'

'South Africa,' responded a clever clogs of theirs.

'Correct.'

I glared at Chris. 'Don't look at me,' he said, 'I told you right.' As it turned out, he did. Jimmy Sinclair, he had great delight in telling me, died in 1913 aged 36 and lies buried in YEOVILLE, just outside Johannesburg. As a slogger, he more than anyone else had put South African cricket on the map. In April 1899 he scored South Africa's first Test hundred with a brilliant 106 at Cape Town against the all-conquering England side led by Lord Hawke. The six he hit at the old Wanderers ground found its way into a coal truck in the railway yards nearby. The truck was hauled to Cape Town by a goods train shortly afterwards, resulting in Jimmy's six being the longest ever recorded.

And blow-me-down, Chris knew an old cricketing tale from Cape Town, too – a

favourite of his dad's, my Uncle Robert. Somerset's Sammy Woods, Gloucester-shire's H.H. Francis, who C.B. Fry described as 'a midget', and C.B. himself approached a Cape Town paddock occupied by a truculent wildebeest – a crea-ture with the hairy head of the gnu and the body of an antelope: a packet of slate-coloured hostility. It stamped its foot and advanced. Francis climbed on the oak gate of the compound, sat on the top, and drummed his heels to tease the beast, which promptly charged the gate like a horizontal bomb. Francis was unseated, and would have been splattered had Sammy Woods, laughing as only Sammy Woods could laugh, not grasped him by the seat of his trousers and lightly recov-ered him.

In retrospect the quiz was the year's low point. By the time we'd squeezed our way into the County Ground a few days later to see Biff's young Somerset side play the touring Australians, Chris had almost been forgiven.

The 50-over match, a forgettable return for Captain Punter, was a sell-out and a never to be forgotten occasion.

Punter won the toss. The Aussies batted first and set a target of 343. They were humbled. The young South African skipper and his fellow opener Sanath Jaya-suriya flayed the Oz bowlers. The pair put on 197 for the first wicket in little over 20 overs. They took 26 off Brett Lee's first four overs with the new ball before he eventually went off with a sore shoulder. Michael Kasprowicz and all-rounder Shane Watson conceded a lot.

Biff smashed his way to a 68-ball hundred. Out for 108, his innings included 17 fours and a six before being stumped off left-arm spinner Clarke. The Sri Lankan import, not wishing to play second fiddle, struck three sixes and was only nine balls slower in reaching three figures, cutting and pulling and repeatedly demon-strating his trademark shot, a lofted cut over point, before holing out to Hussey at long leg for 101 off the Pigeon of Dubbo, Glenn McGrath.

The foundation had been well and truly set, although Hildreth steadied a moder-ately rocking ship after Zum lost the wickets of Parsons and Wood to part-time bowler Michael Hussey. However, with the assistance of reserve keeper Carl Gazzard, and going on to make 38 not out off 24 balls, Hildy saw the hosts to a victory. With 19 balls and four wickets to spare Zum had their first win over the Australians since 1977 when the hard-nut colossus Brian Close did the honours.

Captain Punter wasn't impressed. 'The bowling and fielding was what made me angry,' he fumed.

Two days later, with his Sabres cap on, it was Biff's turn to be cross at the iniquity of Zum, on home turf, losing to the National League Division 2's bottom team Scotland by 15 runs. Zum, for their part, eventually finished 6th in that particular

competition as full attention was given to the Twenty20 campaign. This began in a peculiar manner at Sophia Gardens – a confusing loss to Glamorgan Dragons. The scores were tied at 183 apiece after each side had had their 20 overs. The crowd seemed content with the one point and a tie, but the speaker informed the crowd of the actual result. The Welsh outfit won on fewer wickets down. The match would have its echoes at the Rose Bowl five years later.

As June turned to July a rained-off game and two further losses threatened to deny Zum a place in the quarter-finals before salvation arrived at the County Ground in the guise of Mark 'Boo Boo' Alleyne's Gloucestershire Gladiators. Sabres won by a stonking 95 runs. Biff, Hildy and Donkey clattered and cudgeled Kirby and his fellows as Zum registered a whopping 228 for 5. Man of the Match, however, went to Keith Parsons for his bowling prowess. His 3 for 12 off 3 overs snuffed out the key Gladiatorial batting lights of Spearman, Chris Taylor and Hardinges.

July was also notable for Hildy in another respect. Fielding as a substitute in the Lord's Test during the year's epic Ashes series he had his one notable taste of international cricket, bucketing a second innings catch to dismiss Punter.

Meanwhile, Keith would continue to be instrumental to Zum's cause and play in every match of that Twenty20 campaign. As a witness to what happened he continues to dwell on the incredible galvanizing effects of Captain Biff. I mean it wasn't as if anybody had expected the Sabres to win the bloody thing. But with facial fluff barely turned to stubble, the South African's manner of thought and rhetorical charisma announced him as the Proteus Pericles.

'I've got to say Graeme Smith was the most inspirational captain I played under. He was extraordinary.' Keith eulogized. 'It was a fact that when he left I said to him: "how long do you plan what you say to us every morning?" He said: "I don't. I blow it off the cuff."

'I've heard a lot of captains talks, and I've heard a lot of motivational speakers in the mornings of the game – coaches and captains – but every time we left the huddle that he chatted to, I and the rest of the lads all said amongst ourselves "yer, yer, he's right we can do this". The way he got somehow his message across was just inspirational. He was a very young captain but you wouldn't have thought so. He was very mature. Obviously with his upbringing in South Africa and he came to us as a fully rounded cricketer. I think the way he's led South Africa over the years is testament to that.

'And I think his motivational talks bore fruit right through to the Twenty20 final. We were in that transition time. We had the likes of Wes, Arul, Hildy and Wood, some younger players who came into that '05 Twenty20 side. We scraped home twice against Northampton on route. To be honest we probably snuck up on the rails.

'But we should have lost in the Oval semi-final to Leicester,' Keith admitted. Needing 83 from the last twelve overs defeat had looked a certainty, but then there's that cliché about cricket being a funny old game. The Foxes imploded. They were absolutely cruising when the introduction of Blackwell suddenly turned the tide with the first of his three quick wickets. 'Darren Maddy came down the wicket and slogged at Blackie's first ball, missed it and was stumped by Gazza (Carl Gazzard).'

Indeed, in a match that saw Richard Johnson make his T20 debut, Zum had been exceedingly grateful to Gazza. Him knocking vital runs toward the end of their innings had nudged the Sabres to nearly 160. It seemed a defendable total but barely.

Biff would acknowledge it. 'Getting 157, I thought we'd cooked ourselves and then, especially when they got to 75 for 0, I knew we were struggling. But the key thing was the guys never gave up. In these conditions, in front of big crowds, with big pressure, some of these guys who aren't used to those types of conditions can crack if you keep going at them and they *gave* it to us.'

Paul Nixon's last-ball six was an act of defiance as the Sabres sneaked into the final by 4 runs. Lancashire Lightning awaited.

Mark Chilton the Lancashire captain decided to bat first in hugely friendly bowling conditions only to see Caddy and Richard Johnson destroy the Red Rose top order. And in a piece of fielding that would be applauded in *Wisden*, Wes Durston at point ran out the dangerous Symonds with a direct hit stellar throw. Having stumbled to 41 for 5 the northerners never really recovered despite the best efforts of Aussie Stuart Law that lasted until he, too, was run out off the innings final ball.

Keith was animated as he spoke of an occasion the Oval weather had done its soggy best to spoil. 'They had all the stars – Loye, Law, Flintoff, Anderson, Chapple and Cork. Whoever they had they were far stronger than us on paper. Our bowlers did brilliantly. I think Mal Loye slogged one from Caddy down Jono's throat at deep square. And Jono himself nicked out three. And in a reduced game of 16 overs we were chasing just over a hundred.

'I remember at half-time Graeme was a calming influence. He looked around the dressing room and said: "don't worry lads, we'll be alright here." It was as if he was saying "we've done the hard work. Leave the rest to me, lads. I'll sort it out."

And fair play to him, he did. That's the way he was. He went out and won it by himself with 64 not out, finishing the game hitting Freddie up onto the top tier. Everybody else didn't need to get a lot. I didn't get to bat myself. I was next in. So all in all it was perfect. We won the trophy.'

The margin? Seven wickets with eleven balls to spare. A thrashing. Lancashire, the favourites from the start of the season until the start of the final, had been toppled by a clinically attacking performance. The fielding had been livewire and the brilliant bowling of Andy Caddick, backed up by Richard Johnson, had made the difference. Only Charl Langeveldt pinched from Morecambe Cricket Club and a former warder for the Drakenstein Correctional Centre failed to make any meaningful contribution.

A winner's medal hung around neck, a Man of the Match cheque in his hand, and his red and black Sabre pyjamas made sopping from champagne sprayed and swigged Biff positively beamed. 'This means a lot. I've come in and I feel I've been part of building towards the future,' he effused. 'It's just fantastic to finish off and see the guys perform so well. This is my last day with the team so to walk away with a trophy is special and I'll get on that plane with a really good feeling.'

With the Twenty20 trophy in the bag there was a promise of fresh air around the County Ground. If clouds were gathering they couldn't yet be seen. And if the winds of change were blowing through the Summer Land, especially with Mike Burns retiring quietly, so very quietly, a victim of youth policy, Somerset supporters were yet to feel the breeze.

However, come mid-September the first wafts arrived with the International 20:20 Club Championship, the first notable attempt at a competition featuring the top domestic Twenty20 teams from around the world. It featured the winners of the domestic Twenty20 competitions from England, Pakistan and Sri Lanka, as well as the Leicestershire Foxes and the PCA Masters XI, a composition of current and past players of international cricket from around the world. The winners bagged a princely £25,000. Although being the one and only time this competition particular competition was held, the creation of an international Twenty20 club tournament would be successfully executed with the Champions League Twenty20 in 2009.

Zum's participation in the hunt for more silverware lasted a mere day during which they were required to play two group games. First up were the Faisalabad Wolves at the not particularly exotic venue of Grace Road. Deprived the services of Biff the Sabres had a new skipper. Having plumped for Blackwell, he was sadly unable to prevent an inspired Mohammad Hafeez causing carnage with the bat. In a whirlwind 35-ball 79 he larruped six sixes and six fours. And wanting 10.3 an over from their innings start Zum were never in the game and got stuffed by the competition's eventual winners.

With barely enough time for a shower and sandwich next came a rematch against the Foxes, the self-invited tournament hosts. And for them revenge for the Oval was sweet. 18-year-old keeper Sam Spurway made his Somerset debut and the 66 run hammering Zum suffered was doubly as harsh as that inflicted by the Wolves.

The Sabres, now out with barely a whimper, knew Biff had been sorely missed.

However, in 2012 he was back at the County Ground. So, too, was my cousin Chris. After Trego and Hildreth had helped themselves to tons and got out, he and I looked on in horror at on-field events. Another wicket had fallen but so too had Mark Boucher, South Africa's thirty-something veteran keeper. Biff and his team-mates had anxiously crowded round their stricken team-mate. Photographers clicked away feverishly, among them the young whippersnapper calling himself DavesSCCNews whose image would make the front page of the *Somerset County Gazette*.

Standing up to the stumps, Mark had been wearing a cap rather than a helmet, and had been freakishly struck in the eye by a flying bail after leg-spinner Imran Tahir bowled Zum's Gemaal Hussain. The eyeball was lacerated, the retina damaged. Mark's international cricket career was at an abrupt, excruciatingly painful end. Biff was stony faced.

When play, with grim determination, finally recommenced Chris asked me what, in my opinion, had been Biff's finest Zum moment.

'Leicester,' I said. 'Not the T20 semi-final, but that July's Championship game at Taunton. When he reached his triple century. He scored three hundred and eleven. An innings of mastery.' Chris tapped away at his smartphone.

'Found it, bru.' He whistled. 'Wow, two hundred and fifty-five deliveries, twenty-seven fours, and eleven sixes, what a legend!' More tapping. 'Hey, that gun attack I mentioned? It was in Bermuda. There's a Somerset Cricket Club there, too.'

'Good to know, Chris. Good to know.'

On Twitter AB De Villiers wrote: 'Thinking of you Mark Boucher. Fight like never before my bud. We'll be there for you.'

* * *

TWENTY20 CUP FINAL 2005.
Lancashire v Somerset
The Brit Oval, Kennington 30th July 2005 (day/night)
The match was reduced before play started to 16 overs per side.

Umpires: IJ Gould, P Willey
TV umpire: JW Holder

Lancashire won the toss and decided to bat

Lancashire innings		R	M	B	4s	6s
MB Loye	c Johnson b Caddick	5	5	3	1	-
SG Law	run out	59	45	61	8	-
A Flintoff	c Blackwell b Caddick	2	3	4	-	
A Symonds	run out	12	7	11	2	-
DG Cork	c Trescothick b Johnson	1	3	2	-	
G Chapple	b Johnson	0	1	1	-	
*MJ Chilton	b Blackwell	9	12	15	-	-
AR Crook	c Gazzard b Johnson	15	15	12	1	-
+WK Hegg	not out	6	5	6	1	-
JM Anderson	did not bat					
G Keedy	did not bat					

Extras   (2 lb, 3 w)   5
Total   (8 wickets, innings closed, 16 overs)   114

Fall of wickets: 1-6 (Loye), 2-15 (Flintoff), 3-40 (Symonds), 4-41 (Cork), 5-41 (Chapple), 6-69 (Chilton), 7-101 (Crook), 8-114 (Law)

Somerset Bowling	O	M	R	W	Econ
Caddick	4	0	21	2	5.25
Langeveldt	3	0	28	0	9.33 (1w)
Johnson	3	0	26	3	8.67 (1w)
Parsons	3	0	13	0	4.33 (1w)
Blackwell	3	0	24	1	8.00

Somerset innings		R	M	B	4s	6s
*GC Smith	not out	64	47	58	5	2
ME Trescothick	c Hegg b Flintoff	10	8	15	2	-
MJ Wood	b Flintoff	22	13	12	5	-
ID Blackwell	c Law b Keedy	3	3	4	-	-
JC Hildreth	not out	16	14	23	1	-
+CM Gazzard	did not bat					
KA Parsons	did not bat					
RL Johnson	did not bat					

WJ Durston   did not bat
AR Caddick   did not bat
CK Langeveldt   did not bat

Extras   (1 lb, 2 w)   3
Total   (3 wickets, 14.1 overs)   118

Fall of wickets: 1-28 (Trescothick), 2-60 (Wood), 3-65 (Blackwell)

Lancashire Bowling	O	M	R	W	Econ
Cork	2	0	12	0	6.00
Anderson	1.1	0	14	0	12.00
Flintoff	4	0	33	2	8.25 (1w)
Chapple	2	0	23	0	11.50 (1w)
Keedy	3	0	21	1	7.00
Symonds	2	0	14	0	7.00

Somerset won by 7 wickets
Man of the Match: GC Smith

TEN

Bottoming Out

'For every action taken there is a consequence.'

Alec Stewart.

Somerset had become young, poor disciplined, misfiring and lambent. Summer-landers still wince when reminded of the awful 'Season of Captains' that had begun with Ian Blackwell. 'Zum lions led by a Donkey.' Phillius congratulated himself on his First World War analogy of the trenches. Captain Le Donk's leadership though was short lived. He did his shoulder in early doors and that was him done for. He barely returned to the field of battle.

It was fitting that Matt Wood should be called up to fill the void when fears grew of the wooden spoon. Any lingering veneer of calm was dispelled when Woody quietly reeled under dressing room flak, his voice rarely heard. In desperation Cameron White was summoned from Down Under.

However, although the Victorian captain arrived with leadership credentials he was perplexingly laid back and temporary. So an opportunity arose for durable Andy Caddick to jump into the fray. He wasn't a long term option but emboldened by his obduracy on the field Zum finished with a little bit of something about them, and the Wyvern rag on a pole didn't totally topple.

* * *

Entering through the Jack White Gates there was a whiff of spring in the air as I arrived at the County Ground and headed for the swanky 'Caddyshack'. On the hunt for anecdotes I had arranged a chat with Somerset's Head Coach Andy

Hurry. Morning dew, silvered by weak sunshine, sparkled upon the field of dreams. Not a soul in sight, I mused, before nearly being flattened by a shiny, expensively silent car driven with whoosh by a suited type along the walkway between the family stands and the Ondaatje Pavilion. This was most definitely still the off-season.

The wiry frame of the man they nicknamed 'Sarge' was pristinely clad in his usual T-shirt, shorts and trainers. He greeted me with a handshake liable to crush the juice from a cider apple. Before feeling returned I was led to his sanctum up steel and chrome stairs passed blown up action photographs of his charges – the current crop of first team players. The most dramatic image was of a ginger haired bloke never afraid to sledge pedigree with quips like 'I've seen better batters in my fish and chip shop'. It hung on the top landing opposite Sarge's office. Steve Kirby had been snapped dripping sweat in fist pumping pose, puce in the face, and showing off his carotid arteries having probably just dismembered some bewildered rabbit's timbers.

Kirbs wasn't around, however. Following a path previously trod by Pete Trego in 2008 he was away with an MCC side bagging a 7-wicket haul and victory in the Argentine sun. Thankfully, there had been no reported histrionic shouts of 'Gotcha' at the Belgrano Cricket Club.

Inside Sarge's office, apart from a Royal Marines plaque above the door, the room was without adornment. Sitting himself behind his desk with a military composure that said 'no nonsense' he wrinkled his nose at a mug of tepid coffee. This was the sort of bloke Jamie Cox would have identified with.

I did as bid when invited to 'pull up a chair', yanking at a black, soft-backed, wheelie variety consigned in a corner. It's arm, snagging on an adjacent desk, pulled out an empty draw. 'Room, then, for plenty more player reports?' I flustered. Sarge was taciturn.

To break the ice I reminded him of when he had sprinted in from deep mid-off out of the shadow of the Colin Atkinson Pavilion to catch Sir Vivian Richards in 2003's Lashings charity match. Taunts, the mildest of which had been 'killjoy' and 'spoilsport', had spilled from those appalled in the packed crowd.

Sarge merely declared himself the consummate professional. 'What would you have done?' he asked, imploringly spreading his arms wide.

'Dropped it,' I replied, knowing I would have done so not out of misplaced sportsmanship but rather from personal ineptitude. I looked again at the man who had once made my eldest son blink to fight back water in the eye while those of a weaker disposition wept openly.

After a pregnant pause he told me had lots of things to do, but he'd squeezed me into his day's schedule. And he gave me a warning. 'I've got an intense serious character – facts and figures all the way. You won't get many funny stories out of me.'

So no messing, the ball was obviously now in my court. Well, I thought, best that I took the bull by the horns.

'2006,' I prompted. 'Somerset had four captains and finished bottom of the heap in your first season as head coach. What in gawd's name happened?'

Jaw set, Sarge gritted his teeth before replying.

'The first year of my first two-year contract was a very challenging time, you know. And trouble had been brewing for a number of years. We hadn't developed leaders from within and we'd lost sight of what the culture of the club was all about. There had no vision. No clear direction.

'The core values what makes up this club – the history, the pride of playing for Somerset and pride in the West Country – had gone AWOL. There was no competition for places. Players were journeyman cricketers just going along. And we had no leadership. We were like a chugging ship with a bit of fuel in it. At some stage the fuel was just going to run out.

'I don't know the answer to why the wheels came off, but one of the things a lot of teams struggle with is success after success, so after 2001 it had been building. There were lots of questions needing answers. Had the players peaked? Had they achieved everything they wanted to achieve and then lost their motivation? Were the guys coming through as hungry, motivated and good enough? And what of the signings?'

Now that was the million-dollar question, and a case of 'you win some, you lose some'. New recruit and overseas player at the season's start young Aussie Dan Cullen proved far from an inspiring. Charl Willoughby poached from Leicester showed early promise. And Zum old boy Pete Trego resurfaced with ink-on-blood artwork having spent 2005 in the Worcestershire 2nd XI having failed to gain a contract after short spells at Middlesex and Kent. His return was hardly greeted with a fanfare as 'Tregs' had left Somerset acrimoniously in 2004 and there was little evidence of hidden talent bursting to get out especially as other counties had discarded him. Brian Rose, however, prided himself on spotting talent. 'Dan the Man' was surely a mere blip.

Sarge then voiced his concern that the gap between the best teams in the country and those at the bottom had been too big before asking me if that made any sense. I nodded. Even Derbyshire, the perennial kicking-boys, I remembered had

become the better side. Others, I knew, would put further spin on many of the issues Sarge had raised.

Being a ship without fuel was something Keith Parsons found hard to accept. Certainly not after Zum won the Twenty20 in '05. 'We can look back at tough times,' he reflected. 'It's difficult when you're not winning any games to know where you're headed. Getting through four captains in a year made it tough for everyone. For a young player coming into a side it can't have been easy – never really sure who's in charge, who's picking the side, who's this, that and the other. Nobody really achieved what was hoping for.

'I played fairly well, and other individuals might have done okay, but that's small consolation when, as a unit, things weren't happening.

'I was always someone who was there to win a game. That was the approach I always used. But if you're so far behind when you come to the wicket then there's very little you can do to turn it around.'

True, I thought, unless, of course, you were Cameron White.

On 9 July his brutal 141 at New Road went in vain in the Twenty20. Nine out of ten times when bloke hits a ton within twenty overs his team will win. Not so with Somerset, beaten comfortably by Worcestershire with an over to spare thanks to an equally destructive 97 from Graeme Hick. Cameron's hundred broke the Twenty20 record that he himself had previously held, jointly, with Hick. It took him just 55 balls to register his hundred with 11 fours and three mammoth sixes; the other five Zum batsmen made just 55 out of their total of 198. For Sarge to say 'in that particular game it was our bowling that let us down' morphed him into a master of understatement. Simon Francis went for nigh on sixteen runs an over and Trego, Caddick and Suppiah weren't much cheaper.

Top on the Somerset order that day and only making 6 was that little Aussie left-hander with a kangaroo tattooed on his bum. Justin Langer, over on a six-week watch as cover for Dan Cullen, was getting a taste of the immense task he might undertaking in due course. For their part, Zum could see 'Alfie' being quite a useful asset. In his mid-summer cameo he accumulated his famous career-best triple hundred at Guildford on his only championship outing, as well as more than 400 Twenty20 runs. Consequently, serious discussions were afoot. As Brian Rose had said: 'it's not just about this season but about 2007 also.' Alfie would be a 'wonderful example' to the club's younger players.

And Somerset weren't exactly receiving much in the way of plaudits. 'They were a shambles.' That was Steffan's formed opinion during his first season's stint as a Derbyshire player. He'd arrived telling them that he wanted to earn his holiday at the end of September. 'I want to be sore,' he said. 'I want loads of blisters and

tendonitis. Then I'd know I'd had a great season. If I was fresh come September I'd have had a poor season.' I suspect Somerset missed him more than Sarge would dare admit. And how the Welsh bison bowled against his former employers would have compounded the sense of loss.

Trying to keep his gravitas, Steffan was betrayed by a twitching smile of self-satisfaction. 'We beat Somerset twice in the Championship and I think I got twelve wickets in the two games.

'August's game in Derby was the first at home that Derbyshire had won for over four years. There were big celebrations. Somerset needed 583 to win and got up to 498, but Cameron White got most of those.'

As someone who could hit a cricket ball as far as anyone, he was in Steffan's view 'just a nice, talented bloke'. But 'Bear' showed an aggressive side when goaded. And the Derbyshire game was an example.

'Graham Wagg was bowling when Cameron came into bat,' Steffan said, painting the picture. Oh, gawd, I thought, Wagg the one time cocaine snorter of 'Bearland'. I kept my peace, allowing Steffan to continue his flow.

'And Waggy is the same as he is now, gobby. And he let rip at Cameron. Yak, yak, yak. I bowled to him the next over and he smacked me. And I shouted at Waggy: 'Shut up!'

Even recently Steffan had messaged on Twitter 'keep Waggy on a leash'. That I thought was good and proper given the Graham Wagg masterclass on how to distract a well set batsmen disclosed to *Middle Stump*. The idea when stood close to the batter is to discreetly remove one's todger from one's reach-me-downs. As the bowler reaches the end of his mark let the unmentionable dangle in the batter's field of vision while asking if he wants to see his mum's lipstick.

Given such crudity it wasn't surprising Waggy drove the docile Bear to anger. Indeed, his blood positively boiled. Two hundred and sixty runs later he remained not out – the highest individual score in the fourth innings of a First-class match.

'Bloomin' heck,' breathed Steffan, 'he was unbelievable.

'They messed up really because they were playing nicely. I bounced Caddy and in trying to hook he got caught by Ian Hunter. It was my fourth wicket in the Somerset second innings Then Charl came in, and obviously he couldn't hold a bat. But he tied to take a quick single and he got run out when Somerset didn't need a lot of runs. Had they had better application they could have beaten Derbyshire.'

In Keith Parson's mind Bear would have made 'a great captain' had he stayed longer instead of heading out on Oz 'A' duties. Steffan, on the other hand, wasn't so sure. He described the gurt Aussie as 'a surfer' even though he wasn't, purely because he was 'so chilled'.

Towards the end of this abomination of a season in which Somerset lost an unprecedented nine Championship games Brian Rose knew the need for a shake-down. Things couldn't carry on the way they were. Replacing Bear would, indeed, be Justin Langer to whom Steffan would become both 'the mad Welsh-man' and 'a warrior'. And the batting legend formed a bond with Sarge, too. Together they would follow the mantra: Preparation. Fitness. Discipline.

Few people expected Justin's relationship with Zum to be anything more than the short-term stay originally intended. He admitted at the time that his South West sojourn would prove little more than useful preparation for the impending Ashes Test series in Australia. But then at the end of the 2006 season upon having moved his wife and four daughters to Hatch Beauchamp, about as different from Perth, Western Australia, as two English-speaking settlements can be, he insisted the entire square of the County Ground be resurfaced. 'We would not secure promotion by playing on pitches like this,' he had commented having his new bowling charges in mind.

Head groundsman Phil Frost willingly obliged as bidded, and to hell with the cost.

* * *

Everybody at Somerset, not just Rosey, recognized that the County wasn't good enough. As Phil Frost got on with the square, the club's infrastructure was broken right back down to the bare bones. Chief Executive Richard Gould and Brian Rose the Director of Cricket got involved and worked out first and foremost the need for strong leadership. A motivational, success hungry Langer fitted the bill. He had already seen the prospect the captaincy as an opportunity to make a real posi-tive impact. So that was decided.

The essence of what Zum were about as a club also had to be revisited. What did winning teams do? What was Zum not doing? Where the differences lay and how they could be changed was given for starters to a small working group – senior players, young players, and coaches and the ever-present Gould. The small group morphed into a larger one. After five and a half months of brainstorming every-one was aware of what Zum would look to do.

And pre-season 2007 the alchemy was in place.

ELEVEN

Ups-a-Dazy

'It is easier to go down a hill than up, but the view is from the top.'
Arnold Bennett.

Aided by Marcus Trescothick's self-imposed exile from Test Cricket, Justin Langer sought to quickly turn Somerset's ragged bunch into a team with a winning mentality, and one that could actually win the Second Division of the County Championship.

Justin spent a lot of quiet moments passing the time day with Marcus and was quoted as saying: 'when I played against him for Australia I never liked him much. Not because he's not a nice bloke, but because he's good, and if they're good we don't tend to like them.

'In fact he's an outstanding person, brilliant with our young guys at Somerset, and I reckon England must have missed his demeanour and his example round the dressing room enormously.'

Other notable factors would also help morale. Bear having played the year before with Langer as captain, and knowing Langer was Ponting's right hand man in the Test side yearned to play Test cricket. Making a positive impact on Langer at Somerset was important to him. And then there was Caddy. He, too, aspired to play under Langer. Due to the international adversary between them both, he craved to keep Langer's respect. The young players coming through must have thought: 'this is incredible, this is what it's about'. And so it was.

The County Ground square bore the oblong scars of industry. Frost's had been a thoroughly professional operation. Excavations, more reminiscent of the trenches of Ypres than erstwhile Jonathan Trott style scrapings, trowel and trug gardening or, indeed, conservative scarifying had been painstakingly carried out, fed with loam, and overlaid with the turfs delivered by numerous loaded wheelbarrows. No more dead, flat pitches. Somerset's hierarchy expected results without excuses.

However, after both the Middlesex and Derbyshire had visited at the start of 2007 season, runs were in bountiful supply and the games drawn. In both games sides scored over 800 runs in an innings without being dismissed. It was not good sign. The cricket was, one might say, boring. The hierarchy chuntered as did some supporters. Phil Frost was adamant however that he had told the club officials that the winter's work wouldn't be successful straightaway. Very true.

Records fell.

Against Middlesex, Zum hit the highest score in their history – 850 for 7. Captain Langer scored 315 to add to his triple century the season before against Surrey. Not even Sir Viv Richards managed two triple centuries in county cricket; no other Somerset player ever has.

As for himself, Langer almost exuded an air of contentment. 'Mate, I'd rather play cricket in 50 degrees than 15 degrees.' He spoke from past experience. Somerset wasn't his first county. He spent two years with Middlesex between 1998 and 2000. But he had a prickly relationship with the then captain Mark Ramprakash, who once threatened to banish him from the field following a contretemps at Arundel. At Somerset he was kingpin and just retired from Test cricket, a 5-0 Ashes win under his belt.

No Aussie cricketer was ever prouder to wear the baggy green cap. 'Everything I've learnt about myself and the pursuit of excellence, the places I've been, the people I've met, has been down to the game of cricket. Just a game? For Chris-sakes! It's not a game, it's my whole life,' he said.

As for Derbyshire, well, they managed a mammoth 801 for 8 after losing their first two wickets without a run on he board. Craig Kieswetter on first-class debut had his knee joints and patience tested to the full after spending an inordinate 180-odd first inning overs behind the stumps for nowt but a single catch. Never mind. In the background Brian Rose could think himself fairly satisfied. In addition to establishing an Academy for future generations of home-grown talent Rosey had worked hard to re-establish the county's relationship with Millfield School. Kieswetter was its first ripe fruit.

Come June, things finally started to come together. On a pitch tinged with green

Caddick and Willoughby in tandem put paid to Gloucestershire and this despite a valiant second innings rearguard of 465 from the Shire having been asked to follow-on.

And then came Leicestershire on a further Frost green-tinger. Langer pencilled himself in down at number 7 in the batting order and never got to strap his pads on. The top four – Marcus, Neil 'Toastie' Edwards, Hildy and Bear – all amassed big hundreds. While the bowling of Stuart Broad and David Masters had been utterly ineffectual.

When, aided by Bear's safe pair of hands, Charl Willoughby removed Walker, Leicestershire had been humiliated by the walloping margin of an innings and 259 runs. The end result in the second week of June meant Justin, already having a fabulous summer, had all the bounce of a red-backed wallaby and the grin of a kipper fed cat. And, now back in fold once more and the proud possessor of a first innings 'fifer', the Welsh bison pinned back his ears and hurtled off towards the Ridley Stand.

In the narrow spaces of the little, much loved but slightly decrepit brick and iron stand that gave little room for a cider belly to squidge passed the benches sat the enthusiastic Frost and his groundstaff.

During inert stages of play it was said one could hear the 'tik-tik tik-tik' sound of burrowing woodworm coming from the stand's ceiling timbers. However, there was small chance of such infesting beetle larva being audible over the booming praise lavished by Steffan Jones at that moment. 'Well done, Frostie. That's what I call a cricket wicket!'

The Welsh bison was suddenly having a grand time. 'We were pretty much unbeatable. Probably the best side I ever played with,' he said, putting me in the picture should I have had any doubts. 'I didn't bowl much during the season on return from from Derby. There I bowled millions and got sixty wickets. For Somerset I didn't really understand my role in that first year and just came second fiddle to Caddick and Willoughby. They took loads of wickets. I spent most of my time in the seconds. However, it was fine.'

I prompted Steffan about a certain April event in between the early Middlesex and Derbyshire draws. He beamed. 'Second game of the season? I got a hundred against Leicester at Grace Road.'

'114,' I said chipping in.

'Yep, that's right. Sam Spurway got a duck and we found ourselves 201 for 8. Poor lad got dropped from the side afterwards. Myself and Caddy put on 146. Without those runs we'd have been struggling but we went on to win the game.

'Your 'fifer' at Taunton helped Zum do the double over Leicester,' I reflected.

Steffan puffed out his chest just a little. 'I was the only one to get a hundred and a fifer that year. And it's always amused me that I hit a century before Trescothick.'

Langer was vindicated. Frostie's pitches were producing positive results and Somerset had climbed to the top of the Second Division in the County Championship. In prolific form with the bat, Taunton Deane's temporary resident Aussie was so enjoying himself that summer. 'Mate,' he confided to the *Independent's* Brian Viner between mouthfuls of porridge at the Somerset team hotel in Bristol, 'I say this with the utmost affection and respect, but it's like living in the olden days. At home my life is a whirlwind. I've got my cricket, I have business ventures, I'm on the speaking circuit. Here, everything is slower.'

I asked Steffan to give me his thoughts on Justin. The Welsh bison didn't hold back. 'Hard on the field. Off the field, brilliant. Great family guy. When he spoke in the dressing room you just listened. I don't know if it was the Aussie accent but he had great things to say. On the field he got a bit tense. That's because he had such high standards. Stood at slip he'd been watching McGrath and Brett Lee bowling for years. If I so much as bowled a half volley first ball he'd kick the grass.

'It was hard for me, but I can also understand his point of view of wanting standards. Sometimes it made me angry and got me down. Other times I just thought: "okay, that's fair enough let's rise to it." I bowled some spells over which he'd be the first to compliment me. We were very similar characters.'

'So, you've got a temper, too,' I chuckled. Steffan kept schtum.

During the Glory Years Lancashire members ducked for cover as Sir Viv Richards' bat flew in a shower of glass splinters through the plate glass dressing room window of Old Trafford pavilion, known then as the 'Pit of Hate'. An event for which Somerset later issued a tongue in cheek apology saying that the bat 'had bounced off the floor'. In 2007 Justin's carnage was kept more under wraps following an iffy ell bee. Just let it be said, once back in the dressing room his bat took out its vexation on a very large, very old laundry basket. With the inanimate object finally reduced to smithereens Justin did his best to harmonize the situation. He gave money from his wallet to his wife Sue to go and try and buy a compatible replacement.

My having raised these two events with Steffan his discretion seemed to waiver. 'Langer did go mad when he got out. And he got very angry at Lord's where we'd declared at 50 for 8 first innings.'

'Understandable,' I theorized. 'Middlesex had Zum on the ropes. Silverwood pranged Langer's poles. He got a fat duck, and nobody else really made a helpful

contribution.'

Steffan nodded his agreement. There was no repeat of the Grace Road phenomenon. 'Caddy and me were batting when he called us in. We'd only got a couple
of runs between us when he'd seen enough. And then he had a right go at us
because we'd left the doors open behind us. He was about to really let rip before
remembering himself.

'But I fully understand why he got angry. People cope with it differently and he
had such high standards. He was a stickler for detail and he made the most out
of his ability.'

The Lord's match transpired to be Somerset's only championship defeat of the
season, although in their second innings Steffan managed 64 not out and James
Hildreth a century.

From his office in the Caddy Shack Andy Hurry took a sip of cold coffee and,
becoming contemplative, gazed over my shoulder, out across the square.
'At the end of 2006 we were right down the bottom. We had to get back to being
respected nationally, to rediscover the pride and passion of representing this club.
We had to make sure we created a winning environment both on and off the park.
Everything we did had to be very, very competitive, and it wasn't.

'To go from the bottom to the top was a huge leap. Every club at the start of each
year goes, "yeah, we're going to win the championship" but actually you've got
to be realistic and in fact say "okay, let's reassess what we can achieve in the short
term, let's be in the top fifty percent, and work towards promotion in everything
we do."

Ultimately Somerset won the Second Division County Championship title by a
country mile.

Having gathered enough points already, Zum were already promoted by the time
matters were settled in early September at Chelmsford. They needed ten more to
win the title outright. Essex, though, put up some stoic resistance. Initially the
game seemed destined to be Somerset's. Then, due to the tenacity of leggy Danesh
Kanaria, it was Essex's, before Pete Trego bludgeoned the initiative back for
Somerset, again.

Somerset dominated day one by dismissing Essex for 144 and reaching 284-6.
Only Tom Westley's defiant 72 saved Essex from a total batting humiliation as
Charl Willoughby finished with 5-72.

In reply, Marcus, Toastie and Hildy registered half-centuries as Somerset looked
to build a substantial first innings lead.

All, though, fell victim to Danish Kaneria who claimed all six wickets.

At the end of the second day Zum needed a mere 132 runs to win with nine second innings wickets in hand. The wicket down was that of Marcus, caught off Andy Bichel. Indeed, the Aussie veteran had been doing his level best to disrupt compatriot Langer's plans.

He claimed two of Somerset's the last three first innings wickets and then fired 60 after Essex lost three wickets for eight in 26 balls as Charl made early in-roads.

The match was over before lunch on the third morning. It had taken just 21.5 overs after the day's start. Pete Trego down to bat at number 3 hit 44 off 30 balls and absolutely dispatched Kanaria all over the park, smashing 22 off one over.

Andy Hurry could hardly contain himself as he recalled the blitz. 'These overseas leg spinners can change the game in one over. Tregs was incredible. He took all the pressure off. It was comfortable to watch us win the Championship.'

South African Neil McKenzie, who had only played two previous County Championship matches for Zum as a Kolpak player before his recall into South Africa's Test squad, hit the winning boundary to reach 33 not out as the visitors finished on 184-4. Crikey, Captain Langer and his chaps had wrapped things with more than five sessions to spare. Essex were even deducted half a point for a slow-over rate.

'What an incredible experience,' Andy enthused. 'The game finished about 12.30 and we were just sat outside after lunch with crates of beer on the Chelmsford outfield in a big circle just sharing the moment, and the Essex players came across and wanted to share it with us. It was outstanding. It was a long day because we went to celebrate and it went on right through the night. Sadly for me I'd agreed to do a radio interview at 6.30 in the morning with BBC Somerset. And talked as if there was a badger in my throat.'

Somerset had clinched the title with a game in hand. That game came against Nottinghamshire at Taunton and would highlight someone who'd been knocked around the County Ground for couple of seasons, Zum's legspinning Oxford Blue Mike Munday.

Notts game was very important because they were Somerset's biggest challengers to win the Championship and get promotion. Zum targeted it and worked out long and hard how they were going to beat the bunch of Outlaws.

'We knew how competitive they were,' said Andy. 'They had some international players. They were our biggest competitors but when they arrived in Taunton they'd given up. They'd gained promotion back to the top-flight but they'd given

us the title. I'm not saying they had done, I'm just saying that's how it looked. They certainly weren't the team I expected them to be.'

Zum won. The degree of difference? An innings and 121 runs. It was staggering. Even more so were Mike's figures. He took 8 for 55 in 16 overs against his home county in their second innings that finished after just half-an-hour on day three. His 2 for10 in the first innings meant he also finished with a maiden 10-wicket match haul.

Before the players left the field there arose a poignant and loud applause from the spectators – not for the championship campaign but an ovation for umpire Roy Palmer, the former Somerset all-rounder, who had been standing in his final first-class match from which Somerset had their 10th win of the season. The points haul earned allowed them to finish the season with a record 266 points.

But for a last game defeat to Durham the county would have added the Pro 40 Division 2 title, too. However, Somerset were now back in the top Division of the four-day and 40 over leagues. The Summer Land celebrated. Mooseman, Phillius and I hopped from foot to foot with a merry chorus of 'up-a-dazy, up-a-dazy'.

Captain Langer was already looking to the future. 'I believe we are capable of challenging for the first division title next season,' he quipped optimistically.

The very idea proved exceedingly enticing to a livewire, temperamentally tough, ambitious South African all-rounder. Unfashionable Potchefstroom now well behind him, Alfonso Thomas was in the Potteries – that place of Wedgwood and oatcakes, where everyone gets called 'Duck'. He'd just helped steer Audley to the North Staffs and South Cheshire League title.

TWELVE

Rabbit Heads and Honesty

*'If you truly want honesty, don't ask questions
you don't really want the answer to.'*

Proverb.

2008 was Marcus Trescothick's benefit year. Alfonso Thomas had arrived in the Zum ranks. And the Steffan Jones felt well prepared. Pre-season the Welsh bison had whooshed off to Tasmania before captaining Somerset in a Dubai tournament, returning home as the leading wicket taker. He positively gagged to give it his all.

Mid May, in the Friends Provident Trophy South/West Group stage, he did so. Clad in the Sabres ghastly light blue, red-splashed pyjamas he backed up Captain Langer's ton by bowling the wonder over of his life – a three-wicket maiden. The 'oppo' was Worcestershire. Batty bowled off the first ball. Kabir Ali was plumb ell bee for a golden quacker. Three dot balls to Steffan's former teammate Gareth Andrew followed in a blink of an eye. The last delivery of the over beat the Yeovil lad's inside edge and splayed his stumps. Zum basked in an 84-run win.

Unfortunately, away to Kent, Somerset exited the 50-over competion at Beckenham by 37 runs in June. Originally scheduled to be played at Canterbury the quarter-final affair was switched because of the soggy conditions.

Worcestershire, however, returned to Taunton for the NatWest Pro40 and that *was* a game – a high scoring draw, both sides ending their respective innings son 298 apiece. Daryl Mitchell larruped a four off the last ball of the game to earn the Royals the dramatic tie.

On a perfect batting track, the Sabres knew they needed to set a big target after winning the toss. They succeeded. Their total was built around Kieswetter's 89 – a brilliant knock, made off 82 balls, with three sixes and nine fours.

The visitors, though, looked to be cruising to victory when Vikram Solanki and Steve Davies put on 181 for the first wicket in just 22 overs. But the Sabres stormed back to such an extent that 12 were required off the last over bowled by another the season's bundles of effort; the quite quick though radar erratic, Mark 'Tina' Turner.

In the end Mitchell swept 'Tina's' final delivery past a lumbering Willoughby at short fine leg to level the scores.

The result left both clubs facing the threat of relegation, with Zum in real difficulties. Happily they would beat the drop with a last ditch win over Lancashire by three wickets at Aigburth thanks to contributions with the bat from Arul Suppiah and Carl Gazzard. That said, Zum failed to even get past the group stage of the Twenty20. David Foot, writing in *Wisden,* claimed that too many of the Somerset batsmen had 'lost their way' in one-day white ball cricket.

However, with red Dukes, the Championship lived. Optimism often tends to be an early-season indulgence for Somerset supporters. Even when they finished second in 2001 they did so without ever making it to the top of the table. Which is where, in June, they found themselves. To Zum's fans it felt a tad unfamiliar.

Beyond South Croydon tower blocks, in a refined oasis commandeered by Surrey, tents, marquees, and clipped privet hedges surrounded the picturesque North Field in the grounds of Whitgift School – the posh brick edifice, once home to Lord Howard of Effingham, the Lord High Admiral of the Fleet sent against the Spanish Armada. The school's motto *Vincit qui patitur* ('He who perseveres, conquers') could just as well have been Captain Langer's. Better still, the omens had looked good for him from the outset. Albino wallabies were skipping about – a gift from the Queen, locals bragged.

After perfunctorily completed an eight-wicket win it was Somerset who did the swanking on that early Monday afternoon with heavy rain was forecast. The scores? Surrey 326 and 227; Somerset 446 and 111 for 2.

Captain Langer and Ian Blackwell had both amassed centuries help get Zum into a strong position. Then having done more the hard work on the Sabbath, they had started Monday's play needing to take three wickets and then overhaul whatever slender lead Surrey had managed to establish. 'It was a situation that invited a lax approach and that could have been costly', wrote Andy Bull in the *Guardian.*

Two years previouly, when Zum finished in a heap at the bottom of the Second
Division, the win might easily have eluded them. Now they had Captain Langer.
He admitted after the match that he had been scared when, over the course of the
first hour, Surrey poked and slogged their lead above 100. The second new ball
clipped the innings shut soon after, though, and Somerset needed 108.

Langer thrashed 46 from 30 balls. Usman Afzaal's laid-back left-arm-spin went for
49 in five overs, Langer at one point slog-sweeping him for six into the nearby
Brighton Road. He was out trying to make 22 from Afzaal's final over before
lunch, clean bowled coming down the pitch to try for a third six. He was, he said
later, 'worried about the prospect of rain'. And indeed an hour after play ended
a downpour started. The urgency with which he went after the win was indica-
tive of his tactics for the season.

Marcus Trescothick was 42 not out at the close, having faced 43 balls. Shortly after
he and James Hildreth had trotted off the pitch the team gathered in a dressing-
room huddle to sing a poorly harmonised rendition of the Blackbird.

'I never thought I'd see the culture of a county team change,' Langer said, 'but I
saw it changing here last year.' Blackwell, who scored 158 in Somerset's first
innings and took four for 74 from 30 overs in Surrey's second, had been running
laps at the end of play after he had scored his century. 'I mean, he was actually
doing that,' Langer said, somewhat aghast. 'There must be some miracles in life.'

There were some other diversions, too. The Great Alfonso on a busman's holiday
nipped up to Staffordshire to appear as a substitute professional for Little Stoke
in their home fixture against bottom-of-the-table Barlaston. Trescothick meanwhile had a Twenty20 benefit game at the club he'd played for during his junior
years, although, on paper, Keynsham versus Somerset County Cricket Club had
a one-sided look about it. Despite their smart green caps Keynsham were neither
Australia nor South Africa.

With the remainder of the Somerset side jam stuck on the motorway, Caddy,
putting faith in a Jesus nut, showed off. Attired in T-shirt, jeans, and trainers, the
erstwhile Kiwi landed his little all-black helicopter safely beside the cricket pitch
at Wellsway School. Having settled on terraferma he could only twiddle his
thumbs and wait for his team-mates, including a frazzled Langer, or mingle. He
mingled.

'What big hands he's got,' shrilled a small child in awe, pointing.

Sotto voce, the mum made her own observation: 'what big ears he's got, too. Good
thing he does, mind you, flying that effing thing.'

Caddy unflappable, took the banter in good grace. And Somerset finally arriving

proved a greater distraction. Especially as a BBC 'Points West' news camera crew appeared alongside intent on a partially live broadcast.

Marcus, persuaded to lead the hoi-palloi, managed to restrict a larking, carefree Somerset in grey and red pyjamas to 130 from their 20 overs. In reply, and in front of a large crowd Keynsham through grit, determination and compassion reached the total with 5 balls to spare.

Somerset really should have beaten them. More seriously, they should have also won the Championship. On tenterhooks, even the doubters of Wiveliscombe's *'Bearin' Up'* had actually begun to expect them to. However, they were the quickest to say 'told you so' before guddling away their sorrow. While in his barn, Phillius forcefully wielded a mallet to bash pegs, that I hesitated to think could ever be removed, into a new boat.

Zum had come fourth, 16 points behind winners Durham, after being unable to get a win out of the final three matches. A post mortem was called for after the last of these – an anticlimactic 8-wicket defeat at Taunton to Lancashire in the last glow of September. The plan for Somerset winning a Championship has always been to win away and never lose at home.

Captain Langer who had scored just one more than a baker's dozen sat the all the Club's bowlers, including Caddy, in a semi-circle and one by one asked them what they thought the reasons for the not winning the Holy Grail were. Nobody said anything until, lastly, it became Steffan's go. The poor bloke didn't know whether to speak his mind or not. As it was, and true to character, he just couldn't help himself. The words spilled out: 'Caddick'… 'out of form'…'fifteen overs to take a wicket' … 'the support bowlers were left to bowl with a rabbit's head'. Gawd, that wasn't exactly prudent.

During the latter part of the '07 Championship campaign Captain Justin had singled out veteran seam bowler Andy Caddick, who contributed 70 wickets at a cost of only 24 runs each. 'Absolutely fantastic and a joy to play with' and 'the catalyst for our success' tripped off Justin's tongue. He quite failed to understand why Caddy hadn't been a regular in the England Test side for the previous ten years.

Caddy had become expensive in runs to wickets ratio.

Despite later agreement from Andy himself that Steffan's assessment was correct and messages of support from other players Steffan never played for Somerset again in England. Nor, indeed, did Blackie.

A waistline slimming exercise regime seemed to appall some players. It had been much too tough for the rotund Ian Blackwell. After finding himself in the

doghouse and unable to see eye to eye with his toughie skipper, and also aware perhaps that Justin was something of a martial arts expert, Blackie headed north for the culinary delights of Durham.

'Making this cricketing decision has been the hardest thing I've ever had to do,' he commented, before treading the path previously taken by Sir Beefy, and losing ten kilograms in the process. However, Blackie probably allowed himself a smile at the *Guardian* comment: 'In the time that Langer takes to study the ingredients on a low-fat yoghurt, Blackwell could down a pork pie and a couple of pints of real ale.'

The County Ground became even emptier. John Francis or Keith Parsons both decided to retire. Francis whinged about lack of first-team opportunities, while at the age of 35, Keith, not picked throughout the season, declared that: 'There comes a time when your body tells you it's time to pack in professional sport.'

THIRTEEN

Punch-Drunk, Bear Pit and Lightning

*'Any change, even a change for the better, is always
accompanied by drawbacks and discomforts.'*

Arnold Bennett.

'N'ew season but a familiar story at Taunton, a graveyard for bowlers
and a paradise for batsmen and statisticians,' wrote Paul Boulton in
the *Telegraph* during mid April 2009.

Among the landmarks were a first triple century for James Hildreth, a maiden
first-class hundred by Craig Kieswetter, Somerset's highest score against
Warwickshire and their record fifth-wicket partnership – an unbroken 318 – in
the championship.

Warwickshire's punch-drunk attack was spared further punishment by Justin
Langer's declaration 40 minutes after lunch which denied Hildreth, hailed by the
his skipper as one of the two best young batsmen in England, along with Essex's
Ravi Bopara, the opportunity to overtake Viv Richards's 322 at Taunton in 1985,
the highest individual score made against Warwickshire. Hildreth and Kieswetter were only three short of establishing a record fifth-wicket partnership for
Somerset in all first-class matches.

Hildreth's was also the earliest triple century in the championship, beating
Langer's against Middlesex two years earlier, by two days.

With the River Stand having become a ghost Hobnob could try something new. He
pulled Rikki Clarke for a huge six on to a second-floor balcony on the flats being
built on the town-centre side of the ground. He was the main aggressor but Hildy

applied the punishment when it was required with deft placement and timing. Having completed Hildreth the second double century of his career Hildy needed only 101 more balls to reach 300. A pull off Jonathan Trott for his 35th four took him to the landmark.

On a poignant morning at the end of June Somerset took the field, trotting out from the newly opened 'Caddy Shack' in a Championship game for the first time. Appropriately, Andy Caddick played. Having spring pastured in Clevedon and Wiltshire, he was back in side for his first game of the season. When Yorkshire won the toss and elected to bat a famous name was missing from their team sheet. Michael Vaughan, captain of England's lion-hearted Ashes winners of 2005, had announced his cricketing retirement minutes before the start of play.

Among the straw hats, walking sticks, and broadsheet crossword mutterings, the first tray of pints slopped in the hands of an eleven o'clock drinker. The crowd was building, building. Well, sort of. Two workmen in hard hats leaning on the top balcony rail of the ground's new flats showed no signs of building anything, content, instead, to stump stare.

'This broadcast is brought to you by the Royal National Institute for the Blind,' said the dulcet tone of Richard Walsh, blue short-sleeved shirt and striped Somerset tie to a growing band of listeners both at the ground and listening through internet stream.

Inside our hut it was sweat that streamed despite the best efforts of a whirring desktop fan. We were sat at the foot of the Sir Ian Botham stand looking out across the twin churches from a cramped, flimsy timber-slatted 'potting-shed'.

Semi-retired and armed with binoculars and a pocket *Playfair* crib book Richard was an indispensable. Describing his work as a 'bit of a freelance', on top of his two-hour commentary slot he sorted out the match scorecards, organised the programmes, wrote 'odds and sods' for the *Western Morning News*, contributed to all things Somerset cricket on *Wikipedia*, and did commentaries for the club website's video highlights.

Richard spoke of a 'disturbed' scoreboard, gardening and, all of sudden, chin music. An Alfonso bouncer had cracked a Tyke on the bonce, provoking giggles and a geriatric cry of 'off wiv 'is 'ead' from within the smattering of spectators.

A bleeding ear received attention to the delighted cries of wheeling seagulls. Yorkshire became belligerent. The chimes of Mary Magdalene welcomed Caddy's first ball being thumped into the boundary boards – an early exchange that over four days saw over 1600 runs scored and culminated in a day of brilliance. By its end Yorkshiremen suggested leaving their team coach in a Taunton pub while they returned to plant potatoes in the pitch at Headingley.

Under ever darkening skies the star turn was Pete Trego. He played out of his skin. Coming in at number seven, his clean hitting brought him 6 fours and 9 sixes in 103 not out and a 54-ball century. Tregs' effort enabled Somerset to pull off one of the most amazing County Championship wins in their history by a margin of four wickets.

Zum, though, had cut it fine. They reached their massive target of 476 with 4.3 overs to spare – the second highest successful run-chase in the history of the County Championship. You have to go back to 1925, when Middlesex made 502-6 to beat Nottinghamshire at Trent Bridge to find a bigger winning total by the side batting last in a Championship fixture. And within moments of the players leaving the field there came a cloudburst that turned the County Ground into something resembling a boating lake.

Justin Langer called the victory 'a bit of a miracle', while Peter attributed his dramatic innings to 'a few verbals' from Yorkshire seamer Ajmal Shahzad. He told the club website: 'when I first went in, it was uppermost in my mind to just stay there, because I haven't been in the best of form in red ball cricket. Then Shahzad started winding me up and suddenly the ball turned from a pea into a balloon. I decided to let him have some!'

And so he did, swinging from the hip to record the fastest first class century of the season. With the considerable help of Trescothick and Suppiah, Somerset's effort was the fourth highest run-chase in first class cricket in England and the eighth highest in the world.

At Worcester in July something else phenomenal happened. Justin Langer became the highest-scoring Australian batsman in first-class cricket. He had overhauled Sir Don Bradman's career total of 28,067 runs, going past the milestone with a cover drive for four off fellow Australian Matt Mason.

Not long afterwards Zum cricketers gathered at Taunton Starbucks. 'Good game yesterday,' said the barista 'on bar', to Max Waller.

'Not so much for me. Got tonked and dropped a catch,' confessed Max, knowing that 'sitters' didn't just sip coffee.

'Doesn't matter. It wasn't on the telly,' the barista replied.

Eavesdropping, Captain Langer took his lips from a Cappuccino. 'Oh, yes it does,' he growled. Of course, Justin was right. Values did matter. And he spoke for every cricketing Somerset heart, even the adopted ones. Those in every cow corner and to each compass point of the boundary edge, from Exmoor to Bruton Forest, from the Mendips to the Blackdown Hills.

* * *

North of Frome, evidence of the Viking king Airdeconut had been discovered in astashed hoard of silver found by a metal detectorist in a Lancashire field. There was enough loot to have covered the cost of a reasonable herd of cattle, or a very good herd of sheep.

Come the end of the month the cricketing stakes were a tad higher than that. The winner of the Twenty20 qualified for the Champions League in India, and a minimum return of over three hundred thousand quid. Considering the most expensive sheep ever, a pedigree texel ram, cost £240,000, worse case scenario there would still be plenty of loose change left in the piggybank. Yet, the atmosphere at a sold-out 'Fortress Old Trafford' became highly charged for another reason when the future fortunes of Somerset cricket seemed to turn upon the displeasure of a Norse God.

With the added attraction of overseas superstar VVS Laxman in the home ranks the Mancunian crowds had been supposed to flock in for the quarter-final of Twenty20 'hit and giggle'. But, they hadn't. Not even with brollies. Why bother when the Pennines were as invisible as the Halls of Valhalla? Secretly, the omens for Somerset had been good. Lancashire captain Glen Chapple – missing with a stress fracture of the foot – had handed over to Mark Chilton, the skipper for the 2005 Final.

There was, however, mixed messaging from the *Sky Sports* team. Bumble aka David Lloyd thought Zum didn't travel well whilst still reckoning they would 'win the thing' which on his record of prediction meant Somerset were effectively dead and buried. And Charles Colville made no mention of challenging Sabres when he pontificated Langer and his boys would have their work cut out against the mighty Gurt Red Rose who, so far in the competition, had 'put all comers to the sword'. They were wasted words. Swords, as it turned out, didn't come into the equation.

Lancashire calling themselves 'Lightning' was impudent said some, impishly. And, worse still, to do so wielding pliant willow in the face of Thor, God of oak and storm, was taking the piddle. In order to give those in red pyjamas a reminder who was boss, a 'point' was made over two and half days. The rain descended in stair-rods, each a hammer blow to hopes of play. The grand pavilion once feared by visiting teams as the 'Pit of Hate and the new concrete columns of the skeletal 'Post Box', were mirrored charmingly in the waters of an expansive paddling lake under leaden skies.

Head Groundsman thirty-something Matthew Merchant bemoaned the very wet and trying summer while his sit-on Blotter, having been abandoned beside the drowned boundary rope at cow corner, could reflect on its inadequacy. Everything was far too soggy even for a 5-over plink of 'proper cricket'. After long hours the entire groundstaff team, their hard work wasted, could do nowt but

admire the whiteness of the puddled covers, sup tea and listen to the weather forecast prophesize further deluge.

Old Trafford's excellent reputation for delivering a first-class wicket providing something for the batsman had become immaterial. It was to be purely a bowler's wicket. With both Somerset and Lancashire due to start respective County Championship matches the following morning the ECB had decreed the quarter-final be settled by dreaded 'bowl-out'. The format was simple: five bowlers, two deliveries each, team with the most hits wins a place in the semi-finals.

Umpires Peter Hartley and Tim Robinson temporarily turfed out the kids on summer courses from Club's indoor cricket school, leaving the green floored hall to eerie echoes sourced from a small gathering of journos, snappers, and the odd technician helping provide an on-line video feed for commentary as the wicket was carefully vacuumed to await the teams.

When the Old Trafford pavilion clock ticked round to 1.15, back in the Land of Zum lunchtime ears became glued to BBC Somerset Sound, and mobile phones were tapped to leave personal opinions on message boards as to which five Somerset players should be given the white ball responsibility.

'I wish we had more than just Alfonso (Thomas) as a top yorker man as I think yorkers are the way to go in bowl-outs,' read one. 'I'm going with Alfonso (can bowl good yorkers), Hildreth (bowls wicket to wicket), Trescothick (ditto), Charl (Willoughby) doesn't use his full height in his action so, hopefully, won't bounce it over the top despite being tall man, and, I guess, Arul (Suppiah).'

'I've not picked Pete (Trego) because I think it will swing like a banana in the indoor cricket school,' read another, 'and I've not picked Ben (Phillips) because those indoor strips tend to be bouncy and he's so tall that he would have a job not to bounce it over the stumps, even if he gets the line right.'

And somewhere, somebody became nostalgic. 'Cartwright, Langford, Alley, JC White and 'Budgie' Burgess for me.' This prompted a reply noting the Jones' Allan, Steffan and Adrian. The latter, of course, 'could have knocked all three stumps out of the ground with one delivery. Steff as a 'death' bowler is superb and has been asked to bowl at many a West Wales funeral – ideal in a bowl off. '

And of course there were plenty of other candidates mentioned, amongst them Graham Rose, Andy Caddick, Shane Lee of Wollongong and big brother to Brett, Simon Ecclestone, and that chap described in *Wisden* by Vic Marks as being a member of 'a glittering triumvirate of wrist-spinners who adorn the modern game', England bowling coach 'Mushy' Ahmed.

There was obviously more to it than just holding it cross seam and hoping for the

best. Was I right to assume accuracy rather than speed was the order of the day? A few like me must have thought so after having recently admired Charl Willoughby take a carefree guard, almost standing at leg, against Matthew Hoggard. The former England quickie, in being unable to hit a set of open stumps for a whole over, was testament that accuracy wasn't such an easy thing to achieve, even for the best.

Perhaps in an attempt to confuse their hosts Somerset had Willoughby, Thomas, Suppiah, Mark Turner and the pride of Anguilla, cricket rusty Omari Banks appeared suitably dressed for the occasion. As it was, they finally settled on Trego, Willoughby, Thomas, Phillips and, indeed, surprise, surprise, Omari Banks.

Lancashire meanwhile showed every sign of having flummoxed themselves, which in no small part was due to Sajid Mahmood's radar having gone awry in practice. Their solution was bewildering. The young Twenty20 debutant Steven Cheetham was thrown in at the deep end with VVS Laxman, Stephen Parry, Mark Chilton and Oliver Newby. And, in that order, the 'Lightning' won the toss and elected to bowl first.

Captain Langer with some degree of confidence had his team line up at the back of the hall with arms around their neighbours' shoulders, lending moral support football style.

Eight times Lancashire's nominated bowlers jogged up to the stumps and let fly. Only once did they hit. That was with the first ball, delivered by Steven Cheetham, but he missed with his second. VVS missed with both his, Stephen Parry followed suit, and so did the captain, Mark Chilton. That made it seven consecutive misses, by which time Peter Trego and Charl Willoughby had both hit once and Alfonso Thomas twice, and it was game over.

Alfonso's feat was made all the more impressive by him taking a full run-up. Zander de Bruyn celebrated by breaking ranks and charging down the hall to envelop him in the huggiest of hugs before Ben Phillips could take his two goes. He hit once, but it was irrelevant. Final score? 5-1, proof of Lightning not striking twice, and taking hit and giggle to a whole new level.

Then again, it might have been even funnier if only so much hadn't been at stake. Beating Kent in the semi-final would mean being in touching distance of some very serious dosh indeed. Both the Twenty20 finalists could represent England in the Champions League in India in the coming October.

'Bizarre, wasn't it? I've played cricket a long time, and never been involved in anything like that,' revealed Langer. 'It was a surreal way to win.'

Langer did, however, gently question Lancashire's decision to go with the players

who had proved most accurate in practice, rather than those who do the most bowling in match situations. 'I was a bit surprised Lancashire went with Laxman, Chilton and the youngster,' he said.

'We decided to go with our best senior bowlers, on the basis their action, technique and temperament made them most likely to succeed. But it was all a bit surreal, really.'

For Lancashire it was nothing short of abject failure, particularly for the three professional cricketers who, when required to bowl straight after two days' practice of doing just that, proved unable to do so. Chilton, who like Laxman was anything but a regular bowler, was understandably gutted. 'We knew a bowl-out was a possibility, and we really worked hard on it yesterday, so we were confident in the five bowlers who went up there,' he said.

'We all had a go, and whittled it slowly down to the five most accurate. You try to put yourself under pressure in practice, but it's not the same.'

Thomas, the only man to succeed with both deliveries, was succinct. 'It's a case of clearing your mind,' the South African said. 'After all, it's what we've been doing in our back gardens since we were six.'

There must be a better way a northern voice on the radio said, and went on to question why the game couldn't it have been postponed or moved to a neutral venue at another date. Mark Chilton must have loathed the sight of Somerset ever since 2005's T20 final. Still, credit was due to him for standing up and being counted – or rather not counted.

At the bar of the *Three Ferrets* that evening Phillius passed a tongue-in-cheek verdict on the northern events. 'None of our batters put in any performance whatsoever – I'm not sure they even turned up. It's always the lower order that has to drag us out of the fire, and Zum has to rely on its bowlers to pull us through.' He drained his pint of cider before changing tone to become earnest.

'Even though it was against vacant stumps, winning this one with our suspected weakness is the nearest thing we'll get to satisfying.'

What Phillius had failed to realize was that, counting Somerset's bowl-out success, they had just won more matches in all forms of competition in the 'summer' of 2009 than in any entire season in their rollercoaster history.

* * *

A fortnight later and Zum were in Edgbaston's Bear pit and a win away from the Subcontinent. Happily for his fans, Marcus Trescothick was encouragingly upbeat

about the notion. Touring was what he found impossible at the end of his international career, but before the semi-final he did chat about his personal excitement of the Indian event. Such talk should have made Kent Spitfires, billed as the most complete team on show, very wary.

On a slow pitch Alfonso Thomas continued from where he'd left off at Old Trafford – bowling straight. Four balls into his first over he skittled Joe Denly, and followed it up by skidding one on that trapped Kent stalwart from Klerksdorp, Martin van Jaarsveld, ell bee.

When Papua New Guinea's Geraint Jones was cleaned up by Charl Willoughby Kent were 31 for 3 with the fielding restrictions almost gone and precious time was used up rebuilding. Rob Key couldn't find his timing and the ball off his bat only discovered the boundary twice. From 38 balls he plodded and puffed to 34 before being bowled in an odd fashion when a ball from Trego grazed off stump and required a referral to the third umpire.

It was left to Darren Stevens to provide the Spitfires with some momentum. During the final five overs, he added 52 off 30 balls with Justin Kemp, and passed 50 from 40 deliveries. And the inning's climaxed by Arul Suppiah's left-arm tweaks disappearing for 20 in the final over.

With the Kent attack being more than acceptable, 145 suggested a challenge. But it was one that Trescothick thought to make mincemeat of. He played a superb innings bordering on brutal dominance as he struck 56 off 32 balls, plundering the flight of Spitfires to the furthest reaches of the ground.

Debunking the hop county's excuses that the pitch had made hitting through the line difficult, he took 16 off the opening over of the innings from Amjad Khan with four beefy boundaries in a row. He launched a six over deep midwicket, but saved his best to reach fifty from 27 balls as he drove inside-out over extra cover to knock the stuffing out of Kent.

Justin Langer's 17 runs shored up the other end in an opening stand worth 73 off 40 balls. And he was the first out, getting a leading edge to cover off James Tredwell whose off-spin also accounted for Trescothick – an outside edge to backward point. However, the damage was done, leaving the remainder of the chase a fairly simple affair.

Zander de Bruyn – Zum's leading Twenty20 run-scorer of the season – and James Hildreth found the rope when they needed to and Somerset together with Trescothick could look forward to sacred cows and chapattis.

Kerfuffle and Rumbles

'Nature does not hurry, yet everything is accomplished.'
Lao Tzu (Chinese taoist Philosopher).

The Champions League came off the back end of the Indian Premier League, or IPL, which the world and his dog had been singing about. The excitement and aura that suddenly surrounded Somerset going out to India was in a word, incredible. No one felt the elation more than Andy Hurry. 'It was an amazing feeling on winning the semi-final to know that in getting to the final we'd be going out to this amazing competition,' he declared.

I suppose all sports fans are aware of the Champions League within football and the profile that's associated with it. Well, the IPL was Cricket's equivalent. The only problem was that the Twenty20 finals day had happened in August and the Somerset team was due to fly off in September. Having a rigid timeline in which to accomplish essential tasks generated a frenetic scenario of hurry up before the frustrations of hanging around twiddling thumbs, itching to go.

Sarge had me know that the amount of red tape involved beforehand was 'ridiculous'. The workload for the exotic adventure was suddenly immense for everyone at the club. And it meant both Andy and the cricket secretary beavering away for long hours form filling, visa getting, and a whole other load of 'whatnot'. In short, it was a kerfuffle.

Sorting all the kit out turned into 'a minor nightmare'. A whole different sponsorship layout for the competition was needed. And on top of that, the 30-man squad had to be narrowed down to 15. For Andy tough decisions had to be made

on which players were going to be left behind.

Then his hand was forced and a phone number was sought.

Steffan Jones had been having a tough journeyman's year and was a bit in the background, a bit bitter and had started working at Wellington School on the basis he couldn't play forever. In the preseason nets he'd got Jos Buttler out lots of times but by Steffan's own admission 'he's a bit better now than he was then'. He was loaned to Kent, had pointlessly returned to Somerset, signed for Dorset and got nine wickets in a match against Oxfordshire, travelled up north got nine more in a Lancashire League game, and then Derby beckoned. The Welsh bison was a week away from signing a two-year contract when Brian Rose rang.

'Are you still in to go to India?' he asked. Of course Steffan wanted to go. Derbyshire gave permission and then came disappointment. Zum changed their mind. Steffan understood it was because of Marcus' 'frailties'. Wes Durston had got the nod, instead. An extra batter was needed 'just in case'. Okay fine, thought Steffan assuming that was that. But it wasn't.

Mark Turner had damaged his knee. Last week of September Steffan was back in the frame. He was told he needed a visa just before lunch on the final morning of Derbyshire's endmost Championship outing of the season as they took on Essex in a game of some importance in front of the TV cameras. In Steffan's mind, however, Derbyshire winning and going up to Division One now had a rival in importance – the urgent need to get a visa photograph done.

'I remember panicking,' Steffan recalled. 'I was on the phone to my wife and excited saying "we need visa, we need visas" when bang, wicket gone.'
Out in the middle and on TV Danish Kaneria had begun creating a whole bundle of Derbyshire dither.

Steffan continued readying himself to pop into town.

Bang. Another wicket. Danish was on a hat-trick and instead of jogging to a photo booth Steffan dived for his kit and rushed out to bat with 'no thigh pad, no box, no protection at all.' There was one ball to face before lunch.

'I faced it. I ran off the field, dumped my pads and hurtled out into the middle of Derby to get to get my visa photo done. I didn't have time to grab anything to eat. Once back, I put my pads on again and scurried out to bat with a rumbling stomach. And then we declared. Ten Doescate got 100 in one ball and we lost.

'But the actual trip to India was brilliant.'

Their team finally complete at the eleventh hour Somerset flew to Hyderabad,

the 'City of Pearls' although it's more a city of boulders, whose culture had evolved over four hundred years from when Frenchman Jean-Baptiste Tavernier likened it to Orleans in the Loire Valley. By autumn 2009 such comparisons had become null and void. The breathtakingly ornate minarets of the Charminar were surrounded by a congested, heaving colourful mass of Haleem and Biryani munching, ghee greased, street life.

The local city market was as raw as India comes – spices, teas, flowers, clothes, you name it and they'll get it. In pockets of waste ground, and with stumps cobbled from bricks, concrete blocks or metal drums, kids thrived on improvised games of cricket. All about them the air had the carbon perfumes of buzzing Tuk-tuks and the static jams of cars and lorries because of flyovers, and heaven knows what else, being under construction. Skyline offices of Google and Microsoft dwarfed towering billboards. And sprawling shopping malls declared 'shop, eat, celebrate'. It was a different world to Somerset where the tallest building in Taunton was Debenhams and biggest mall, 'The Pig Market'.

Zum had a police escort laid on from Rajiv Gandhi International Airport to their hotel because the Hyderabadi loved their cricket so much. Sarge had been flab-bergasted. 'We were treated like royalty. It was incredible, absolutely incredible. We were treated like gods. Driving to our hotel you may have seen a million people on the side of the road living on a blanket but when the gates opened to the hotel and you could have been in Vegas.'

In a reception provided by the hotel staff the foreheads of the whole Somerset entourage from Captain Langer to the support staff were each smeared with a bright red bindi dot, said to retain energy and strengthen concentration, and were gifted garlands to self-consciously wear around their necks in honoured welcome to India, the Mecca of world cricket.

Locally it had begun back in the 1930s when teams with such names the Free Looters and the Retrievers attracted the likes of Jack Hobbs and Herbert Sutcliffe to play alongside Professor D.B. Deodhar and Vinoo Mankad in the Behram-Ud-Dowlah Tournament. Performing horses were kicked off the gymkhana ground and matting wickets laid. As the most important event in the local cricket calen-dar all offices, colleges and schools, declared a holiday, Maharajas, Nawabs and Rajas entertained teams inside their tents and shamiyanas, and in front of piled assortments of bicycles, five deep standing crowds ringed the boundary.

The romance had, however, morphed. Caps gave way to helmets, amateurs became professional, and cricketers attained a status to rival the Bollywood stars from Hyderabad's film studio, the largest on the planet.

Steffan loved it. Well, the hotels anyway. 'I barely set foot outside the hotel in Hyderabad. You'd go down the street and there were cows sat in it. And you'd

look up and there wouldn't be any front walls to the houses and you could see a person on the toilet. And we'd think "what have we come to 'ere!" Then you'd get into the ground and they all wanted to touch you as we practiced and prepared for the Deccan Chargers game.'

The Chargers were the IPL Champions and they were on their home deck. Having won the IPL in South Africa this would be the first time they had played in front of their home crowd since being crowned champions.

Steffan remains rueful about the great event. 'I bowled really well in all the warm-up games and I was the leading wicket taker. But when the first proper game against Deccan arrived I wasn't selected. But I could understand why. Had I done brilliantly people would have asked: why isn't he playing for us next year? Wes Durston was another unfortunate who'd be released. But I had no gripes. It was just a brilliant trip.'

Fate had it that at the time I was in India, too.

FIFTEEN

Tea and Salutations

'Come, let us have some tea and continue to talk about happy things.'
Chaim Potok (American Jewish Author, 1929–2002).

Calling itself a 'retreat', the place I had found myself was run by a cricket despising married couple in a cricket mad country. It felt like being in an internment camp. Sans wifi, the accommodation did, however, boast a small TV. Sadly, poor reception and lack of any live sports content made it next to useless.

'Gordon Bennett! Love, will you look at this.' I called my wife Ali over to the offending object. Despite a snowstorm of fuzz the pictures were undoubtedly of the County Ground in Taunton. We were nearly five thousand miles from home and we were getting the local news. A thirty-something Indian gentleman wearing a necklace as tight as a garotte was being interviewed. 'Murali Kartik joins Somerset' wobbled the caption. His contract would be considered generous. Amongst its terms Zum would be obliged to buy a bicycle for his wife – just the thing for taking in the fresh air and the tractor riddled, high banked, narrow, twisting muddy country lanes overgrown with cow parsley, prickly nettles and snagging brambles. How far away it seemed.

Bless her cotton socks my wife Ali had been impressionable. For seven years after yoga's damned introduction at the County Ground she'd harboured ambition. And in 2009's off-season I finally comprehended that Shakepeare's term 'kicky-wicky' was nowt to do with an incensed bowler reacting strongly to his butterfingered stumper. To the Immortal Bard it had the valid meaning: one's nearest and dearest.

Crows cawed. Chilled to the marrow and enshrouded in dawn mist I could well

have been catching my death on the Quantocks. But I wasn't. Diplomatic towards Ali, I'd found myself on a hilltop without an apple tree in sight, high in the tea growing hills of Nilgiris in Southern India where the British had built their empiricist hill-stations Ooty and Conoor. Here ladies in colourful cardigans and supporting sacks plumped fat with freshly picked tealeaves on their heads waded waist deep through the tea plants back to the Homedale Tea Factory.

My limbs had been contorted, and muscles I never knew I had pained. If that wasn't enough, there were the added discomforts of daily pummeling and the non-cricketing runs. Life had become a drastic slimming diet of Ayurvedic cooking shored up by heavy massage, medicinal potions, Ganesha mantras, and hardcore yoga.

I craved my local butcher's melt in the mouth lamb chops, and healthy venison bangers, not to mention the meat pies which had they been discovered by Ian Blackwell before his move to Durham would possibly have made him spherical.

So, contrary to feeling relaxed, I felt defeated. Like Virender Sehwag singing to himself when batting, oblivious to statistics, I, too, was in a world of my own trying to keep my spirits up during purgation. Playing *Howzat* dice cricket helped.

Ali remained stoic. 'We're in this together. Don't be a whinge-bag. You can still give your moral support to the Somerset boys. They aren't far away.'

True, taken in context, I suppose they weren't. They were five hundred or so miles away up north, fourteen hours by train if very lucky, three days or more if not, living their life of fidgety royalty cooped up in their Hyderabad hotel with a match day dawning.

On the morning of October 10th, my hair slick with pungent massage oils and my body and clothes reeking from the stuff, I'd skived off the yoga, leaving the more supple international souls to their sun salutations. A problem needed to be solved.

Later, after dark, Langer's Sabres were set to play the IPL Champions Deccan Chargers. It was an historic occasion giving me goosebumps. Mighty Zum were one of England's two representatives in the inaugural Champions League competition.

The Sabres, the Twenty20 Cup runners-up, had qualified despite receiving an incongruous 63 run mauling from the Sharks inside the Edgbaston Bear pit where a calypso innings of 59 from Barbadian journeyman Dwayne Smith took the game away from Langer's chaps good and proper. Now, both teams were in the mix with ten others – the great and the good of India and those having flown in from Australia, New Zealand, South Africa, and the West Indies.

Each and every one of them was $100,000 better off, less expenses, just for turning up. So, worse case scenario, all Zum had to do was play a couple of games in the

group stage and 'Kerching!' With three teams drawn in a group they had found themselves plonked in with Trinidad and Tobago, winners of the Stanford 20/20 of 2008 who had a bloke in their side called Kieron Pollard, and, of course, the Deccan Chargers.

If the Sabres managed to get the wood over just one of the two then, in likelihood, they would make it through to the League stage of the competition. Should they manage that then a further $100,000 was guaranteed to be coming their way – more than enough to fritter away during the hours spent in Starbucks and Nandos without hurting the purse strings.

It was all to play for. The Chargers led by the grizzled veteran of bygone Ashes Adam 'Churchy' Gilchrist were first up, and I felt helpless. The resort's management had two draconian rules. Firstly, no guest shall fraternize with staff. Secondly, no guest shall leave the resort after dark unless management is told exactly where he or she is going.

Stuck where I was how could I possibly follow events when there was no easy escape route to the cyber cafés of local civilization? I mean to say, a taxi would draw attention and public transport was tortuous. A steam train to make the locos of the West Somerset railway look new-fangled did puff up and down the mountain, but on an infrequent schedule; whilst tuk-tuks, though as common as hunger, were careering, phutting, jolting, three-wheeled abominations of hang-on-for-dear life inshallah machines.

Anyway, slipping passed the front gate in cow corner was a teaser in itself. His uniform sharply creased, the handlebar moustached ex-soldier cum general factotum passed muster as a sentry. Being of the see-all-say-nowt type he might have qualified as a Yorkshireman but from his desire to collar anyone he heard to be English. Once snared, he'd rabbit loudly in earshot of the resort office about the exploits of Freddie Flintoff with an extent of knowledge worthy of winning *Mastermind*. He was aided and abetted in gate duty by an obstructive companion – a watchful black and white cow that provided milk for daily urns of masala tea, understood only Hindi, and liked nothing better than to moo loudly and nuzzle you with slobber.

Having extricated oneself troops of annoying monkeys would intercept incipient pedestrian progress to Conoor. Break their cordon and several pot-holed miles of serpentines with rickety buses often dispensing rear window pellets of vomit lay ahead. Then at the first roundabout stood the army barracks where nosey soldiers took sport in waggling guns.

My only realistic option had to be the resort's 'library' – in reality no more than a few shelves of dog-eared tomes containing not a word of cricketing comfort – which boasted a dusty PC.

Melbourne Shaun, a scary, emaciated Aussie, his knitted woolly tea-cosy hat pulled down over his shaved head, but not low enough to hide the vicious tick in his left eye, was hogging the electrical artifact connected by dial-up to the outside world. This was no fan of his local team the Big Bash's Victorian Bushrangers in Group D. Indeed, he hadn't shown the slightest inkling of understanding towards a cricket fan at all.

How nice it would have been to discuss the achievements of a character in common. Like say Bear, a star of Bushrangers as well as Zum.

'Err-hum,' I coughed as politely as my patience could bear. No response. 'How long you gonna be, chap?'

'Dunno, mate. Anyway, Roopa's after me.' His tick became the viciously bog off sort.

I dutifully picked up the stub of chalk to scratch my name on the adjacent blackboard only to be aghast by the list of names hailing from Brazil, Mexico, Turkey and Austria that had already 'booked-up' the whole evening until well after the last ball would have been bowled in the Rajiv Gandhi International Stadium.

What to do?

I headed for the kitchens watched by a gardener tending his vasa and vibitaki herbs while a bee-eater hovered, poking its curved beak were it wasn't wanted. And a brown bird about the size of a hen blackbird puffed itself up and squeaked as though it were a child's toy amid an unending stream of migrating monotone dragonflies flying in thousands passed the open kitchen door. Inside, Chaggi the young cook sat cross-legged on the floor peeling a papaya breakfast, listening to a tinny radio glued to his ear.

He waved. 'Mister Charles, your Marcus Trescothick is playing tonight! They've just said so. I hope he doesn't get the jingly-jangles.'

'Me too,' I said. For all his problems Marcus, in his first game out of England in a while, was apparently due to open. This was great news for optimism. Zum surely needed him. Banger was one of only ten Englishmen to score a white ball hundred in India.

Eureka! The radio! How to follow the game in Hyderabad had potentially just been solved. 'Chaggi are you here this evening?' Looking at the gurt piles of 'healthy' vegetables surrounding him in need of peeling that was something highly probable.

'No, I'm going to my friend Vipin.'

My bottom lip rose over my top.

'Oh, Mister Charles you want the cricket!' chuckled the observant young cook. He reduced his voice to a furtive whisper. 'You could come to visit Vipin, too. He's rich and has a television. Better still he can afford STAR cricket.

'And please bring your wife.'

Thank goodness for that, I had a hunch it would've been grounds for divorce to leave her out of this evolving scheme.

'How do we ...?'

'Don't worry Mister Charles, Praboo owns a tuk-tuk.'

Not knowing whom the hell Praboo was, or whether to laugh or cry, to me there was one certainty – the shenanigans Chaggi blatantly suggested could get him the sack. But despite such fears a plot was hatched. Inshallah mode it was to be. Chaggi assured an hour after the crow multitudes had flown overhead back to their evening roosts when the gods turned down daylight's dimmer switch the front gate would be unguarded. The sentry would be in the kitchen having his evening meal, reading the sports pages of the *Hindu Times*. The cow would be tied safely to a tree.

* * *

Unbeknown to me there was an incredible amount of nervous energy floating around the team bus on the way to the ground because this was one of the biggest games any of the guys had played in their lives.

'You could feel the atmosphere,' Andy Hurry recalled. 'The noise was deafening – something not new to international players of experience like your Trescothick's and your Langer's who'd played out in India. But there were probably thirteen players in my squad, and certainly five support staff, that had no idea what to expect.' And the Sabres certainly weren't expecting what they encountered.

'Obviously, we were organized,' said Andy, as if I ever doubted him. 'We talked about our plans of how we were going to do things. We did everything we could do off the park. Of course we talked about the noise and having visual cues rather than verbal ones. But we didn't anticipate just how loud it was going to be. We walked out onto the field and stood more than three feet away from someone you couldn't hear what they were saying. It was so loud it was ridiculous. I mean, the stadium wasn't even full but the atmosphere and noise was incredible.'

* * *

Headlights! Like Charl Willoughby edging a 4 to release his creative juices I felt we were on a roll. Ali, always up for things spontaneous, stood beside me, staring into the pitch black at an approaching twinkle accompanied by the increasingly audible sound of a tuk-tuk's straining two-stroke.

Fifty yards from us the lights stopped moving and went out – cloak and dagger stuff.

Hand in hand we moseyed over. 'Praboo?' I asked the silhouette in the driver's seat.

Wobble of the head.

'You're taking us to Vipin?'

Another, wobble of the head.

Formalities over we got into the back seat for a throw-around hysteria inducing adventure. I presumed it was Praboo at the wheel. The full-throttle two-stroke roar made questions impossible. Saying that, with our hearts in our mouths we could only groan or giggle nervously. Had we been totally stupid?

I decided to distract myself by trying to recall Zum's 35 official captains starting in 1882 with Nailsea's Cambridge Blue turned London schoolmaster Stephen Newton up to and including Alfie.

I got as far as Brian Close, one of the few, along with Sammy Woods, John Daniel and Brian Rose, to have led Zum over 200 times, God smiled upon us. Suddenly halting the tin trauma by a kerb in Heaven knows where, 'Praboo' gestured us to follow him on foot.

Led into a manmade labyrinth I hummed *Mad Dogs of Englishmen*. Feeble light spilling from windows into narrow alleyways cautioned trip hazards of loose stones, tree roots and irregular steps. Finally, our guide leaving us with nothing worse than stubbed toes melted back into the dark. Hurrah, we'd arrived.

Home for Vipin turned out to be two rooms with bare concrete floors. From what I could make out, one doubled-up as a rudimentary kitchen and bathroom in which two young women in saris fried batches of banana fritters and boiled a copious amount of water. On a small table were a couple of dozen tin mugs. The other room heaved in a hot, sweaty, airless fug. A happy chattering bunch of men and boys were crammed-in. From the middle of them Chaggi grinned at us. There was just enough space for a rolled up mattress and a pair of empty pink plastic chairs. On the wall a large shelf supporting a nifty state-of-the-art TV, along side it was a shiny poster of Indian cricket idol VVS Laxman, leaving no doubt which team was being rooted for on the night.

Born in Hyderabad and educated at the city's sweet sounding *Little Flower School* this one-time medical student had blossomed. Set to opening the batting with Churchy for Deccan he had the worrying potential to carve up the Zum bowling attack. Sambit Bal had commented: 'At his sublime best, VVS Laxman is a sight for the gods. Wristy, willowy and sinuous, he can match – sometimes even better – Tendulkar for stroke play.'

Palpably, VVS' batting was more accomplished under pressure than his bowling. I bowed my head towards the poster in gratitude acknowledging a root cause to Somerset actually being in India could be traced back to him twice missing the stumps twice in July's famous Old Trafford T20 quarter-final bowl-out.

Vipin gave me a nudge and pointed Ali and I towards the chairs. 'Please,' he said, 'You are my guests.'

Self-conscious, we trod carefully through the arm and torso jumble managing to ensconce ourselves not a moment too soon. An explosion of Hyderabad fireworks announced the players taking the field of the Rajiv Gandhi International Stadium, capacity 55,000. Umpires Harper and Koertzen were experienced enough not to be unnerved. But would Zum wilt under the pressure? This was a far cry from the intimacy of Taunton's gentle heckling. In addition to Laxman and Gilchrist the Chargers had the likes of Andrew Symonds, RP Singh, Chaminda Vaas and Fidel Edwards. Zum had their work cut out for them.

'Fingers-crossed those Langur monkeys don't cause us a problem, tonight,' said Vipin squeezing himself in at our feet.

I frowned down at him. How ungracious. Vipin insulting the cider boys surely wasn't cricket. 'What do you mean "Langer monkeys"?' I asked, revealing an edge of tetchiness amidst the room's expectant hubbub.

For a moment Vipin seemed puzzled. Then light the dawned. 'Oh no no no, Mr. Charles. L-A-N-G-U-R. They can be such naughty pitch invaders.

'What you need is a mug of black tea,' he laughed. 'It helps the stress in times of cricketing importance. Chaggi's ayurvedic wisdom. I always have some brewing when Very Very Special has a good chance of a century.

'Oh look your Justin Langer has won the toss. Sadly, I feel it's the only thing your Somerset will win tonight.'

'I'm sure Langer has a master plan,' I retorted, none too confidently. Well, whatever plan he did have started with him pleasantly inviting the Chargers to bat first on what Gilchrist would describe as 'an absolutely beautiful wicket'.

First up, Langer tossed the ball to Willougby. Was that a half smile on Gilchrist's face? Zum's fielders shouted encouragement to one another and clapped their hands. Here we go. Up to wicket trundled Willoughby, jaw set, eyes steely and bowls. Willoughby's walloped. Four! Crowd noise ramps up. The South African wiped his brow, gave Churchy the eyeball, and tried again. Four! Then, out of the kindness of his heart the Chargers skip clipped a single allowing VVS the strike.

You don't use adjectives like hammer and clobber to describe shots from Laxman but straight away he almost batted with a touch of violence. He charged down the track to Willoughby, cleared the front foot and heaved across the line. Four!

Doubtless the Great Alfonso would have better luck. Not so. Dismissively, Gilchrist nurdled one. Back on strike VVS scratched his nose, moved outside leg and flat-batted a length delivery back past the startled bowler. The Chargers were off at a gallop.

'Chai!' shouted Vipin into the kitchen.

With Churchy having cracked a six our tea duly arrived at the start of Thomas' second over with the Australian eyeing mid-wicket. In Alfonso bustled and banged the over's second ball in short. A little late on the shot Churchy miscued his pull. Top-edged, the ball lobbed up towards gully. Trescothick trotted a few paces forward to complete an easy catch. 35 for 1 and much celebration from Zum, and also from the pink chair. Vipin took a big slurp of tea.

Langer thought this a timely moment to introduce 'Bus' aka Ben Phillips into the attack. VVS gave himself a couple of sighters before edge hoicking Bus to the fine-leg boundary and a giving him a sheepish smile. Lady luck was riding with the Chargers. With a wiggle of his mug Vipin requested a top-up.

Ruthful, Langer decided Bus warranted a slip and beckoned Trescothick.

Attempting to clear mid-off Suman drove hard. Edged! Banger leaped like a River Barle salmon to snaffle the sharp chance. Suman, gone, out for half a dozen! 59 for 2. Wonderful Bus! Zum were truly in the game as the temperamental Aussie Andrew Symonds strode to the crease, the stadium now having more of the Bull Ring about it than Birmingham, his original birthplace. A lot was resting on 'Trigger' Trego to apply the squeeze, whereas Symonds obviously had it in his head to force the pace.

'Run Hildy, run!' I exclaimed, urging James Hildreth in from long-on. Oh, just the ticket. Symonds had toe-ended a tonk straight into Hildy's palms. A wicket for an excited Trego and the Chargers at 78 for 3 were slowing to a canter.

Five balls later they were reined into a trot. Trego let go a slow off-cutter bowled

full on a teasing length. VVS' eyes lit up. The Indian maestro tried to swing the delivery over square-leg but the poor chap was too early on the shot and missed. There was a collective gasp in the tiny house in Conoor as white leather shattered the timbers. I swear Vipin squeaked.

'Ooo, that was good Darling, wasn't it?' stage whispered Ali, asking of my opinion. Inwardly, I knew it was very, very good. Outwardly, I stayed shtum and merely nodded, a smile twitching at the corners of my mouth. Best be British and not to show too much ecstasy.

Chaggi, though, was a mind reader. Fast as a whippet, around he turned from the TV screen. 'I know what you're thinking Mister Charles,' he said with mock gravitas. 'If Somerset win, then tomorrow morning I will make a special breakfast of spicy bread to show there are no hard feelings.'

A score of 88 for 4, VVS out for 46 off 35 balls with 7 fours, I don't suppose, was really in Chaggi's or Vipin's plot. Their tea was left to go cold as Deccan crawled from 86 for 3 in 10 overs to 99 for 4 from 15 overs as Rohit Sharma and Scott Styris tried to rebuild the innings all over again. Zander de Bruyn with his dibbly-dobblies did his bit to apply the pressure resulting in Rohit finally losing patience with the penultimate ball of the fifteenth and holing out to Alfonso in the deep. He was quickly followed back to the pavilion by Styris, as the Kiwi, trying to drive through midwicket, was struck on the pads. Harper didn't take long to raise his finger. 'Rubbish, umpire! That was going down leg side!' Vipin was indignant. I tapped him on the shoulder. 'Any more tea?' 121 for 6.

In at number 7, Venugopal Rao had three left in which to throw the bat. He did so with good effect clobbering 22 off 12 balls. Again Willoughby suffered. Bus meanwhile landed one in the block hole getting an on off to peg back Singh's stumps, before Rao, in trying to clear long-on for a third time, could only loft it out to Hildreth in the deep. Zum picked up a ninth wicket, that of Ojha in the last over, run out by a Thomas/Kieswetter combo to leave the West Country men a chase of 154 to win on what was adjudged to a good batting surface.

Vipin blew out his cheeks before confidently declaring: 'I think we have enough runs.'

'We?' I queried before announcing the urgent desire of Ali and I to get some fresh air. Everyone else seemed content as they descended upon a large stack of crispy battered bananas as another gallon of hot tea brewed in hope.

Enter Trescothick and Langer. Fidel Edwards was volunteered first use of the white cherry. Two crunchy Banger upper cuts and joy of joys Zum were off to a flyer. Then catastrophe. Singh enticed Banger into pulling a little too early. Top edge virtually straight up towards the heavens! Gilchrist calmly set off to his right in anticipation of gravitational pull, and judged science perfectly. OUT! Ten balls

of the innings gone and Zum were 16 for 1.

De Bruyn joined a watchful Langer, and together they kept the scoreboard ticking nicely. Zum's 50 arrived without further alarm. Singh, however, put the cat amongst the pigeons. Making room to thrash him through point and cover, de Bruyn got a thick edge, Gilchrist dived full length to his right in a manner befitting a Yeovil Town goalie, and snapped a majestic catch prompting the crowd, and all but in two somewhere in Conoor, to go doolally.

Calming down, Vipin shared some wisdom. 'Catches win matches!'

Two balls and one run later and I was witness to pandemonium. I could see what Langer tried to do and that was to clear mid-off. Problem was, he didn't. Rao gratefully pouched the offering. Zum were suddenly 51 for 3.

Foolhardily, I put my faith in Hobnob and Trigger knowing they'd target Pragyan Ojha the spinner. Oops. With one tossed up outside off, down the track came Hobnob to swing hard and make an absolute horlicks. He hadn't got completely to the pitch, and swatted it straight to the perfectly positioned long-on who didn't have to move. 59 for 4, and we were already in the ninth over. By the middle of the eleventh things got worse. Trego holed out getting more elevation than distance. Between them the two middle guns had amassed just 17. Half the side was out, Zum had lost 6 for 49 and Vipin was shouting 'chai!' again.

To be fair, I thought my host had read it right. Before it could exit the nineties Zum's batting had all the crumble of an ill-kept cob wall. Tempted by Ojha tossing the ball up, Suppiah threw prudence to the non-existent wind and went for the slog-sweep. This time it was Styris watching the object of desire into his palms at deep midwicket. Then Bus tamely chipped Suman to Symonds at midwicket leaving the equation 55 to win off 6 overs with only three wickets left. And it started to drizzle.

For a spell Langer and Gilchrist furrowed their brows, beguiling themselves checking the Duckworth-Lewis equation.

Meanwhile, looking determined, the Great Alfonso had joined Hildreth in the middle for a chat of intent. From then on the game became really quite thrilling – to the extent of being on the edge and then out of one's pink plastic chair.

A destructive 13-run over off Pragyan Ojha in which Thomas hit a six and Hildreth a four turned into a 50 run partnership. What a couple of heroes. The maths came down to nine from 10 balls after Thomas paddle-swept RP Singh over the short fine-leg fielder. When a yorker ran for three leg byes it seemed the game was done and dusted, but foolish me for thinking it so. 5 runs were needed off the last over. Deccan heads had dropped. The crowd had been tamed into a defeatism

infecting the lovable bunch around Ali and myself. From the kitchen one of the ladies shrilled something in Hindi. 'My wife will be very cross if the tea gets wasted,' translated Vipin despondently.

'I will remember your breakfast,' confirmed Chaggi with dignity.

In truth Deccan had probably been undone by a damp ball that needed toweling and by an unfortunate faux pas from Fidel Edwards sending down his second beamer first ball of the 17th over. Lack of grip, probably. Yet, rules were rules and he was taken out off the attack.

Gilchrist had to gamble. Styris was given the short straw of bowling the final over. He gave the ball a good wipe. 'C'mon, Hildy,' I muttered. 'Just one big hit.... oh, God.' The stumps were in disarray. Couldn't blame Hildy. The notion to make a bit of room to smash the orb over midwicket was sound. His bat simply failed to make contact.

'Okay, Max next. Perhaps this was his time. Worryingly, however, young master Waller, former Millfield School cricket captain, looked a tad bunnified with nerves. His first delivery from Styris was met by a sound defensive prod. Well done, fella. Now having acclimatized it was time to hit the bloody thing properly. Fingers-crossed. 'Oh, Lor!'

Hit it he did – a miscue. Attempting a slap back over the Kiwi's noggin, the ball didn't travel far but did go high enough for the batters to cross, allowing Alfonso the strike, before Styris celebrated an easy-peasy caught and bowled. A moment conveyed by the gurt scoreboard. It read: W 0 W.

Happy undecipherable banter was collectively directed at me as Chaggi and his pals went slightly potty. 'See, that's why Deccan are IPL Champions!' pronounced Vipin, doing a daft jiggle. Tea was spilt.

Nine down, and in came last man Charl, trying his level best to look businesslike, wheeling his willow like a dervish. Heads in hands Ali and I weren't fooled. Zum had capitulated.

Alfonso, redoubtable Kolpak, surveyed the field and readied himself. Full toss! Sliced! FOUR! 'Oh, Alf, you little beauty!' I extolled over the sudden deathly hush. The scores were level and a mid-wicket conference between the Deccan skipper and his bowler ensued. Whatever was agreed worked.

Dot ball. So it was down to the wire.

Last ball of the match, Deccan fielders all on their toes saving one, and in from his short run bundled Styris. The delivery produced was excellent – a teasing full pitch just outside off stump. Adrenalin fuelled, Alfonso played the shot of his life.

Beautifully carved. FOUR!

What a rollercoaster. Hot, mentally exhausted but totally elated, I expelled words that I'd prefer to describe as 'oil beef hooked'.

Magnanimous in defeat, Vipin found the perfect excuse to absorb the post match interviews by saying: 'I think we need one last mug of tea to all calm down.'

* * *

Although left virtually speechless a euphoric Alfonso managed to stutter a couple of sentences together: 'I can't believe I have done that. It's still not making sense … I just had Peter Trego saying he can't hug me enough.'

Justin Langer was more phlegmatic, crediting the squad being a tight unit as a key factor in their success. 'That is one of our advantages. We're coming off a lot of county cricket and have had a couple of fantastic years,' he said. 'Ironically, we've won a lot of close games like this so it is a great tribute the character of the club. For most of our guys to play in front of a crowd like this and in an excellent stadium was a great thrill, and then obviously to win a very close contest goes to show the character of the club.'

* * *

After our protracted goodbyes and sworn oaths of friendship Conoor was finally left a cluster of twinkling lights behind up as Praboo zoomed Ali and I safely back to the resort. Drunk on self-satisfaction I felt neither lurch nor bump believing that in Hyderabad Somerset's cricketers sang lustily about that blackbird in a Wurzel tree and a great big stick to knock him down. I would later discover this to be true, and by several accounts also to be the happiest moment of Justin Langer's illustrious eighteen season first-class career.

There was, however, one downer. As we nonchalantly strolled through the front gate well before midnight there was a reception committee waiting. The resort's owners stood, arms folded, appearing miffed.

'Salutations. Here you both are at last.' The wife glanced pointedly at her watch. 'Shane saw you leaving and kindly informed us,' said she. 'I want to know if you've been associating with any members of my staff.'

Ratfink Aussie snitch, I thought. 'No, we haven't,' Ali lied, making her cheeks burn.

The woman's eyes narrowed as she scrutinized us. 'We've been worrying about you. Don't you know how dangerous it is out there?'

'Yep, I can honestly say we thought it fit to stop off to admire a load of Sabres,' I said.

In tandem the husband and wife team looked horrified. 'Well, well ... don't do it again,' admonished he.

Gawd, I reflected, you cricketing lads with your fancy hotels and careful diets, can never know what Zum folks go through to give you their moral support. But for Sarge and his yoga I'd certainly never have been provided with such an authentic atmosphere in which to enjoy it.

'The Deccan Chargers game will be right up there for the rest of my life,' Sarge told me, 'because it was the first chance for the majority of the people associated with the club to be involved in such a game against such high profile players. And from that experience I felt: you know what? We're not that far away. One of the things we talked about internally – it wasn't an external thing – was that we aspired to be the best in domestic World cricket.'

After the conclusion of the Chargers game, albeit fleetingly, Sarge could boast that they were.

* * *

Somerset Sabres didn't win another game during the 2009 Champions League although their victory against Deccan Chargers was enough to qualify them for the league stages of the tournament eventually won by New South Wales Blues who defeated Trinidad and Tobago in the final.

In helping his team finish runners-up Kieron Pollard included an innings where he scored 54 runs off 18 balls. This not only earned him an IPL contract at the 2009 IPL players auction where he was sold for an undisclosed amount after attracting the maximum possible bid of $750,000, it also attracted the speculative eyes of the Somerset's Director of Cricket, Brian Rose.

Probably thanks to monies earned in the heroics of Hyderabad the scent of lucre was wafted under Polly's schnozzle to entice him to Taunton for 2010. Nothing ventured, nothing gained, wise heads said.

He would pitch up to discover Somerset had dropped their Sabres tag. That was no great loss given there could be no more sarcasm about Zum 'losing their cutting edge'. Anyway, it was a silly name. Based, it was said, on a committee member stating categorically that cavalry sabres used to be manufactured somewhere in the County. Something my friend Phillius had feverishly trawled the web unsuccessfully to disprove.

But habits died hard. 'Glawster' would continue to have the moniker printed on their tickets and BBC Radio Bristol would still refer 'the Sabres' in sports news.

SIXTEEN

No Panic Just Despair

'All our best heroes are losers.'
Richard Glover, radio presenter.

New to Twitter, Phillius had put the whisper he'd heard in his quiet corner of the Quantocks out into the world. 'Stroppy Aboriginal limpy joins Glawster'. This led to a moment or two's head scratching on my part until I read a Glos Cricket Fans tweet that made matters clearer. 'Dan Christian signs for Gloucester March 2013'. So Captain Klinger had his Redback team-mate joining up with him. I wondered what was going through their mentor's mind back in Adelaide. Doing so definitely gave the story a wider West Country angle.

Somerset hero Jamie Cox, now ensconced as South Australia Director of Cricket, may consider sending the Shire a postcard of advice about buildings and contents insurance.

Fair to say, Dan, who in '09 led a touring team of Aboriginal cricketers to our shores, had in November '12 been offered anger management counselling after he became the bane of dressing room plaster on three occasions – Adelaide Oval, Blundstone Arena and the WACA – after being dismissed.

'When blokes get out it really is tough,' Coxy said. 'But it doesn't give anybody the right to actually smash up equipment and smash up dressing rooms. We all have bad days but you can't go belting holes in walls.'

What Phillius expressed in his tweet had been succinct, but blatantly he still hadn't got over Somerset's T20 final loss to the hogs in 2010's mid-August day of

soggy wet balls that marked the flow of disappointment and tears.

And last ball of the match and with one run needed Zum hadn't shown the slightest inclination to actually run out an excited Dan hobbling through mental aberration the full twenty-two yards to come a worthy second to his runner.

The umpires were patient for long enough to each read a novella cover to cover but sensing a West Country disinterest in the laws of cricket called game over and removed the bails themselves. But what if Zum had run out Dan? Needless to say he'd have been a tad cheesed off.

So one can't help but think Dominic Cork and his men in custard yellow owed unending gratitude for Zum ignorance that helped preserve the fabric of the Rose Bowl.

'That cap, black eyes, Hobnob's skittles, old Nick, and that Christian,' had been Mooseman's summing up the culmination of the year's t20 – a competition that had seen Alfonso Thomas win so many 'Man of the Match' cheques that, he joked, they paid for his pristine Audio TT.

'That cap' became a serious debating point in the final clutching at straws. In the fifteenth over of Zum's innings a wallop from Hobnob had seen the ball plug just short of long-off before rolling over the fielder's cap as he scrambled for the sphere. 'That's five penalty runs, ump,' shouted an indignant West County voice. The knowledgeable umpires Bailey and Illingworth conferred but didn't give them, believing the cap contact wasn't deliberate. Zum fans everywhere dusted down their rulebooks convinced they could prove the officials wrong. But no, penalty runs only arose if the cap was 'willfully' discarded.

As an aside, it would have been really helpful to Cameron White, him having been surplus to requirements and twiddling his thumbs in Taunton's Castle Hotel, had the Somerset committee looked at their rulebook, too. Being charitable, there had been something of a misunderstanding. Yes, counties were allowed to field two overseas players in the Friends Provident T20 but Somerset, who already had Pollard and Kartik, thought that meant they could field Bear as a third, so long as only two overseas players actually took the field for the side.

The ECB felt compelled to intervene. And it categorically declared that a county could only have two overseas players registered at any one time. Eating humble pie Brian Rose had to tell Bear of the boob and apologize. Bear could do little other than have a grumble, gather up his clobber, and return to Oz.

Responding to a question posed by a committee member as to how much 'Beargate' had cost the club, Richard Gould glibly replied: 'A couple of thousand. He is a friend of the club.'

But anyway, back to the final. The black eyes mention by Mooseman belonged to Dan, who looked like a panda having been hit in the face by a ball by Zander de Bruyn a couple of days earlier, and Kieron Pollard, who had his right eye closed by a Cork short-pitched, game changing, brutish snorter. So instead of finishing his innings and having a bowl at Hampshire a bleeding, swollen faced Polly had to be carried from the field and whisked off to hospital. Later, at three o'clock in the morning, he was found tear-stained in his hotel room, sobbing he had let 'everybody down'. Bless him, had he been able to see for himself he would have known this to be untrue.

During the chaotic ten minutes of the match's last over bowled by Zander Somerset had several opportunities to win yet took none of them. Craig Kieswetter played skittles thrice and despite having eternities to take aim was agonizingly awry each time. Compo Dog, snatched pre-season from Middlesex 2nd XI by Brian Rose, spilled a boundary catch, a blessed sitter. And Panda Dan pulled a muscle.

At Hampshire's request the groundsman was summoned to mark out a runner's crease. 'Whitewash! Whitewash!' announced Bumble to anyone who could hear him. On to the field the groundsman trotted, a bucket in one hand, and in his other he clutched a piece of straight edge timber and a brush. The artistic distraction gave time for Panda Dan's pain deadening adrenalin to kick in before the final ball fever. Zum clutched briefly to hope as the ball stuck him on the pad. Replays showed it to be clipping the leg stick, a legitimate ell bee shout in life's umpiring lottery. Umpire Bailey surely could have lived with himself for giving it out. Instead, the crowd was treated to the charge of the custard panda.

The rest of the Hampshire custards running cock-a-hoop onto the field before the leather stopped rolling technically made it a 'dead' ball. Noticing this Mooseman apparently did his best towards getting Somerset a reprieve by screaming at umpires Bailey and Illingworth: 'the hogs are on the pitch! The whole Hampshire team's on the bloody pitch! They're not allowed to be on the pitch! The match isn't officially over! Umpires!' He was absolutely right. Unfortunately the umps were keeping their peepers on whether or not Zum fancied running out Panda Dan, and Mooseman's protests went unheard as he was ranting at his sitting room telly.

Assuming wrongly that Zum knew the law that a batter with a runner should stay put in his crease or face being run out, the award for the most inane comment of the season had to go to Sky Sports 'on the mike' Ian Ward. 'I don't think Trescothick wanted to win that one. Not that way.' Someone should perhaps tell him Marcus, by his own admission, continues having recurring last ball nightmares.

The day had other noteworthy highlights. Polly's leaping catch at long on to knock out Notts in the semi-final was probably the best snaffle of 2010. And then

there was the hilarity of the fire alarm going off in the BBC radio commentary box that caused Alison Mitchell to commentate via roving mike from the terrace of the stand sans headphones with many a tuned-in spectator waving at her, including six giant bananas doing a conga beneath the scoreboard assisted by Snow White and seven Grumpies. The way Ms. Mitchell prattled on I could have sworn her sympathies lay with Hampshire. But at least Frampo had won his wager with Marcus.

Andrew Frampton of the internet radio station *Farm Radio* bet that if he got on the pitch at the toss on that Finals day Marcus would in return open the new pavilion of Frampo's local village team in Dorset. Come the toss and much to the Somerset captain's surprise Frampo made his appearance. Looking very official dressed in a smart blazer and carrying a clipboard having hoodwinked the Rose Bowl security he reportedly whispered in Marcus' ear: 'here I am – now you come and open our pavilion.' It certainly wasn't a bad idea. Trescothick would have discovered somewhere he could hide.

However, it was the County Championship and the desolation of what might have been that caused the greatest heartache and a regret that had tentacles beyond the South West, as I discovered the time I was in Bridgwater after Lancashire had won the 2011 title.

I had been 'People Watching' – a low key sport offering a way of passing a bored hour or two on a grey Saturday when an aspiring cricket writer has a book signing appointment with a disinterested public.

Through the plate glass window of the *Bridgwater Bookshop* the street side local throng weren't the average cricket crowd – the pierced, tattooed and shabby, the brisk suited types looked busy with loosened ties and undone top buttons, the pallid honey monsters dragging on fags and tugging at tantrum toddlers whilst pushing prams, the weather-beaten farming types taking time outs to lift flat caps and mop brows, and the Barbour jacketed horsey faced yah-yahs playing elaborate dodgems. From out of the mix and into the shop strolled three happy chattering splashes of vibrantly dressed colour. Unmistakably, northerners on holiday: parents with a teenage daughter in tow.

'We saw the poster in the window and thought we'd come in. What's all this about, then?' asked the mum, casting smiling eyes over the table laden with book copies.

'Somerset cricket,' I replied, doing the hard sell.

'Is it full of funny stories?'

'Some say it is … in parts.'

The dad picked up a copy, skimmed through a few pages and then nodded to his young lass who in turn tapped at a pink iPhone and pressed 'send'. 'We'll see what Darren says,' he said.

As we waited for their social networking to function I learned that actually they were family members and 'down from Preston'. Mum had left Somerset thirty years ago just as the pomp of Zum's 'Glory Years' ran out of puff and James Hildreth had been a twinkle in the afterglow of 1983's NatWest victory celebrations that had dimmed long before young guns like Kieswetter, Buttler, Dibble et al were conceived.

The mum became wistful. 'I've come home.' She gave her hubby a kiss on the cheek. 'But my heart's now in Lancashire.'

'You here to gloat, then?'

The iPhone beeped.

'He says we should have one.'

'Blimey, that's good news,' I said. 'Is Somerset his second favourite county?'

'Not really,' said the mum a little sheepishly, 'it's just that he still feels guilty and embarrassed.'

'Hmm. Nottinghamshire 2010?' All three nodded, and I scrawled my illegible signature into the book. The small royalty, I decided, should be charitably donated to Depression UK. Supporting Zum can leave one feeling starved and stuffed, leaden and denied.

On September 16th the Championship's last evening, a rheumy-eyed Brian Rose had tried to point a brave face on his desolation at Chester-le-Street. Durham, Ian Blackwell et al, had forced a draw while Lancashire capitulated to Notts. From somewhere a Lancashire supporter blogged an embarrassed 'Sorry' and stated his intent never to renew his club membership.

Stuff could have, nay should have, worked out so differently. Things had begun to get really exciting when Lancashire were the visitors for Somerset's last home Championship game of the season. Aging Somerset members sensed the extraordinary happening in their lifetimes. Like cats on hot bricks, coins jingling in their pockets, they made queues in front of Taunton car park ticketing machines before finally being able to leg it. Many gripped onto sun hats and walking sticks for dear life as anticipatory and jaunty they scrummed towards the Sir Vivian Richards gates or other points of entry. The Championship dream beckoned and, just to be greedy, there was the Clydesdale Bank 40 final to also look forward to.

Sod the Rose Bowl, now. Amongst the herd I, too, was sprightly, infected by the mood of that heady late summer.

The growing tension was apparent in the Somerset team. 'The guys are well aware of the history of the club and never winning the Championship,' Marcus had told BBC Somerset before adding that old chestnut about still having 'a massive mountain to climb'.

In the match itself all appeared to be going to plan as Somerset built a first innings lead. During a last wicket partnership between Murali Kartik and Charl Willoughby under oppressively black rain threatening clouds the lead extended to 123. Murali hit his second fifty of the campaign. Charl, too, hit some lusty blows, including the flattest of sixes, prompting him to later tweet 'I will be a proper allrounder if I get to 1000 1st class runs and 850 wickets!' Then eighteen runs shy of to a fifth batting point Charl was run out while on what can only be described as a meandering ornithological survey of seagulls. 'Ooer,' commented an affable Red Roser standing beside me. 'That dropped batting point might prove to have been useful. Ey oop. Lanky-Lanky-Lancashire!'

'I think what mattered,' I said, giving him a nudge to interrupt his flow, 'was losing our first two games of the season. Then again if we cider boys do win the title, due thanks must be given to Jacques Rudolph for his quixotically generous declaration here back in May. Us chasing down 360 within 66 overs kind of put the Tykes Championship hopes on the back-burner.'

'Whatever. I only came today to watch Chanderpaul bat.'

Others wanted to watch, too. About to start his two-hour stint of duty stood in front of the Old Pavilion steps but behind the canvas sightscreen a grey-bearded safety-steward friend in a floppy summer hat rather dilly-dallied. He wished he had a pair of scissors about his person to cut a small hole through which he could eyeball the unfolding drama.

As it turned out Shivnarine Chanderpaul didn't last too long. Alfonso Thomas claimed his wicket and it was key to Somerset winning the match. It also earned him a prize – a choice of one of Marcus' bats. 'I went over to his bat corner before the season started and asked him what I had to do to get one,' said Alfonso told the local press. 'He said get me one hundred wickets and you can take your pick.' The gifted West Indian falling ell bee took Alfonso's tally past the hundred mark in all competitions for the season.

However, it wasn't the prospect of a beautiful bat that pleased Alfonso most. 'If you'd said to us at the beginning of the season, two points behind with the last game to go I think we would have chopped off both arms really,' he had enthused. On hearing this, and having witnessed the great Alfonso being caught by a Sky

Sports camera on the Somerset balcony dragging on a fag, Mooseman confided in me, that the chopping the arm off business might eventually come regardless if the whippet-like bowler didn't quit his naughty smoking habit.

The Championship though had become a three horse race between Somerset, Yorkshire and Nottinghamshire. All three were playing up North. Somerset though in addition had booked themselves a CB40 final berth thanks to a 95 run win over Essex fort-eight hours prior to beginning their vital four day game at the Riverside.

What had happened before The Fates conspired that Shivnarine should edge to a gleeful Samit Patel at slip, signalling a helicopter to whisk the Championship trophy to Old Trafford, lay recorded in my Moleskine.

* * *

Monday 13 September.
11.00 am Rain in Chester-le-Street or Concangis as it once was. Haunted No Ordinary Hotel' Lumley Castle looms ominous. Cricketing clientele claimed to have witnessed paranormal activity. So spooked were the Aussie's in 2005 that all-rounder Shane Watson is reported to have slept on Brett Lee's floor. Five years earlier, three members of the West Indies team checked out of the same hotel because they, too, had the heebie-jeebies. 'There were a few funny goings-on,' said their captain Jimmy Adams, 'but we put them down to Franklyn Rose running around under a bed sheet.'

3.25 pm Play underway.

Durham 132 for 2 at close.

Evening. Brian Rose, Vic Marks and Somerset President Roy Kerslake dine at the *Fat Buddha* a restaurant of Asian fusion offering 'high design and unique atmosphere'. They discuss Twenty20, the acquisition of Steve Kirby from Gloucestershire and drainage.

Tuesday 14 September.
11.00 am Somerset supporters are getting excited – some have planned to jump on flights to Newcastle. BBC forecasting the following for the next 3 days:
Manchester – 2 days of rain.
Durham – SUNSHINE FOR 3 DAYS! GAME ON!

2.30 pm Third bowling point and Somerset lead the county championship table by one point – clear skies over Chester-le-Street. Sodden outfield prevents play at Old Trafford.

Set of rain clouds heading inland from Welsh coast. If a biblical storm were to arrive on these shores and wipe out all cricket from now until Thursday night Somerset would be county champions for the first time.

2.32 pm Ben Phillips traps debutant Raul Brathwaite lbw. Durham 286 all out.

4.48 pm Bad light and late afternoon rain.

5.00 pm Durham Scoreboard switched off, scorer gone home.

5.15 pm Scorer probably has to U-turn in rush-hour traffic. Tresco and Compton restart the Somerset innings.

6.05 pm Somerset lead Championship by 2 points. Pete Trego tucks a single off his ribs.

Somerset supporters from Toronto, Daar al Salam, and Instanbul blog they're going potty. In Bejing a supporter was teaching flatmates 'Somerset La-La-La' in basic Mandarin.

6.10 pm Ian Blackwell – hands in pockets, two sweaters, looking absolutely perished rubbed the ball to polish it and drops it. In Manchester Notts have only managed to reach 89 for 2 after two days.

Wednesday 15 September.
11.00 pm Blue skies in the North East. Somerset resume day three on 226-4.

12.55 pm Ben Harmison traps both Jos Buttler and Ben Phillips ell bee to the last two balls before lunch.

1.40 pm Rain stops play.

2.10 pm Players back on.

2.30 pm Hildreth pulls Liam Plunkett for four. Hildy's 100! Great advert for Mill-field School. His 7th century of season and he gets married within the week.

2.38 pm The Great Alfonso nurdles 3 runs. Somerset 400-7. Maximum batting points. 6 points clear at the top! Somerset become the first team to score 400 at Chester-le-Street in 2010.

3.05 pm Alfonso has his timbers tickled by Ruel Brathwaite. Somerset 423-9.

3.11 pm Murali Kartik skies a catch to Ian Blackwell to bring the Somerset innings to a close. The leaders are 426 all out and lead by 140. Tea.

6.00 pm Durham 171-2. Di Venuto hinders Somerset's victory push. Close. Somerset 8pts, Durham 5pts. Zum have gleaned all the bonus points possible. But docile pitch – first designed for the ODI between England and Pakistan last Friday. Durham batting spirited and professional.

Notts still frustrated by the Manchester puddles. No play during day. Contrivance feared. Huge Zum gratitude if Mark Chilton and Peter Moores could ensure that Lancashire are at their most stubborn.

'Stuart', a Notts supporter clutching at straws blogs the following: 'what are the ethics, rules or laws around Notts and Lancashire concocting some sort of result? Personally I'd be up for some skulduggery, but I'm the sort of bloke who doesn't walk when he nicks it.'

Thursday 16 September.
People are excited – some have jumped on flights north. Standing out with his sideburns, ruddy cheeks and cider mug Somerset's most loyal of supporters Tractor Driver, sporting 'Mr. Driver' on his T-shirt, was among one of a couple of dozen Somerset fans who had travelled 275 miles, as the crow flies, from Taunton to see a potentially historic end to the championship season. Tractor had put great distances under his belt over the years. 'From the naughty north to the sexy south, we're all singing – I have the mouth!' as he puts it.

11.15 am Manchester: Notts batting after a delayed start,
Headingley: Yorkshire 130 all out second innings. Relegated Kent need 90 to win. Come on the White Horse stamp you authority.

Lunch.

Durham and Notts still batting. Kent wobbling. Tyke title?

Tea.

Kent beat Yorkshire by 4 wickets. Now two horse race.

Somerset mop up the last three Durham wickets for 26. Title delicately poised. Zum need 181 to win off 17 overs with Marcus and Kieso in their arsenal.

Debutant Ruel Brathwaite handed the new ball by Phil Mustard and Trescothick edges the first delivery straight to first slip. Field in one-day mode, Michael Di Venuto at two-and-a-half slip.

Spinner Blackwell opens from the other end. Maiden (although there were three byes) against his former county. Pressure tells. Kieswetter plays a big yahoo to his second over, and loses middle stump. Blackwell has bitten the hand that used

to feed him.

Trescothick drives to Borthwick at extra cover. An ugly swipe and Trego's stumped by Mustard. Blackwell again. Game up.

4.11 pm Damage limitation time. Zum battened down the hatches.

4.35 pm Manchester: Notts hit 311 runs in the squelch closing their first innings on 400 for 9. 5 batting points. Sugarplums!

Zum needing 133 from the last five overs shake hands on a draw.

I bite nails.

Zum's pennant dreams now hang on the bats of the Red Rose top order that haven't picked up a bat in the match so far. On the positive side they only need to survive a handful of overs, well 16 as a bare minimum. Somerset still win title even if Lancs lose a couple of wickets. Please God don't let them lose a third.

5.00 pm A portable sponsorship screen is set up in front of the Emirates Durham main stand in readiness for presentations. Despite the draw, Somerset have perhaps done enough.

5.10 pm The big screen is showing Notts take 11th hour wickets. The presentation kit is quietly being folded away. Andre Adams is the anti-hero, grabbing the second and third Lancashire wickets. Nottinghamshire 'edge it' with forty minutes of the season remaining.

6.30 pm Blog: 'As a member of Lancashire CCC all I can do is offer my sincere apologies for our spineless surrender today, sad to say it's not the first time it's happened this season. All in all a gutless batting exhibition. Less than 5 overs to lose 3 wickets. Sorry. Somerset had a right to expect something better.'

* * *

Had 'Stuart' the Lancashire fan been merely mischievous? Nottinghamshire had sneaked the extra bonus point they needed to finish the season level on points with Somerset, and claim the £500,000 prize money by virtue of more wins.

Out there on the web 'Rural Idiot' commented: 'I think that the match at Old Trafford was contrived, Notts scoring 400 – 9 and then Lancashire 11 – 3 in just 4.4 overs. Come on it's just a bit too convenient and looks like a Pakistan result.

'If I were the Somerset club I would be asking for clarification about what happened at Old Trafford, it stinks.'

Poor Marcus, it wasn't just the castle that had a haunted look. He had to endure a maiden Championship title quest unravel in the cruellest of manners while he and his team watched and waited on the pavilion balcony. 'It's gutting, with it being our first we realise how special it will be when we finally get there, he lamented. 'To get so close – level on points – is so tough but we'll just have to wait another year now.

'It's terrible. It's something that will live with us for a long, long time. To know we were so close, touching distance to the trophy, but so far away when Notting-hamshire got that third wicket." Yes, he spoke haltingly in platitudes. The true emotion lay in his reddened tear glistening eyes. No one had expected the Old Trafford result and Trescothick admitted that up until the near end they had actu-ally been watching Yorkshire.

I asked Andy Hurry to analyse the Durham game from the benefit of hindsight. 'We achieved our aim,' he said. 'We bowled them out. We got runs on the board. There's a minimum amount of time left and were having to score 14 an over, or something ridiculous, and we thought right we're going to go for it. We win the game we win the Championship. We've got nothing to lose. We can't lose. We're not going to get bowled out in which case we take all our draw points. Then it was dark, Durham put everyone out on the boundary, the ball was zipping about off the moist deck – it was an impossible challenge. We couldn't control winning the Championship ourselves.

'So the game finishes all eyes go to Old Trafford. Their game still had half an hour to play as our game ended early so we could get to Newcastle airport to fly down to London for the CB final on the Saturday.

'They had the 400. Okay, no worries. To win it because they'd won more games they still have to get three wickets to get a bowling point to equal us. To equal us! They ain't going to get 3 wickets in 25-minutes, we thought. Then all of sudden Lancashire are like a pack of cards. They seemed to roll over.

'It's a phenomenal story really. You can't say county cricket's boring. The emotional drain I can't put into words. On the plane I swear nobody talked to another the whole way. People just couldn't get over it – to have come so far and not got it when it meant so much to everybody.

'We've all experiences death in our lives, that's the serious end of the emotion scale. The other end's euphoria. We were somewhere towards the serious end. It really was a feeling of total emptiness.'

To their credit Durham played the game hard despite having no chance of honours or even prize money. In the end Somerset paid the price of not having quite enough penetration in their bowling attack. But can any county side ever

have lost two trophies in one season both by a tie-break? With that sort of record in mind one rather expected the Clydesdale Bank 40 final to be relatively close affair, too.

In the bar of Taunton's *Pitcher and Piano* Mark Turner had been catching up on old times with Graham Onions whom he had been at school with when the 'D-word' was whispered – 'Derbyshire'. He would be leaving after the final. Not just Somerset but also Keith Parson's Taunton St. Andrews, would miss 'Tina'.

The final question was: would he actually play? Max Waller was the alternative, and chuffed to still be on the Somerset books, had got his hopes up of getting a game. The Lord's pitch had been assessed and was thought to be a turner. Max, though, had misconstrued. Mark Turner played. Although 'a bit pissed off', Max could only shrug and admit that Somerset cricket was all about being part of a squad. However, the selection decision came to bite Zum on the arse.

Somerset completed the most unwanted of trebles in front of just over 14,000 – a small crowd by Lord's final standards but far more than had been feared. The lead-up time to the final had been short and both sets of supporters faced tricky journeys home. The match finished after the last trains to their respective parts of the country had departed.

Trescothick found the 'gutting' defeat hard to bear. 'We're proud of what we've achieved as cricketers this season,' he said, putting on a brave face. 'We've been probably the most consistent team through the year, and we've put ourselves in a position to win three trophies. We could be talking about a completely different situation, but obviously we're not.'

The reality was that, well as Warwickshire played, Somerset had manoeuvred a winning position upon batting first after Marcus lost the toss. Having reached 173 for 3 with 10 overs to go, however, they crumpled.

A gormless run-out – when Compo Dog called through Hildy for a run that was never there – torpedoed a promising partnership and opened the door for the master of legbreak googly, Imran Tahir. Having bowled four largely fruitless overs from the Nursery, Bell switched him to the Pavilion End to produce one of the most remarkable bowling spells a Lord's final can ever have seen. He took five wickets in four overs for just 14 runs and Zum were all out for 199 like the clappers. It was never enough.

The heroic bowling efforts of Ben Phillips had been in vain as Warwickshire centurion Ian Bell, recovered from a foot injury sustained on England duty, saw the ball like a beach ball. After being bowled on a free hit and surviving a close ell bee appeal from Murali Kartik, he had the measure of a fired-up Somerset attack and hit 107 to guide the Bears home.

Tina was especially picked on. Not only was he leaving Zum, he also went around the park as Bell took 20 from the match's third-last over. What had looked like being a close finish in the first county final at Lord's under lights became absurdly easy.

For the Somerset supporters it had been a tough week, both mentally and physically. But what of the cricketers?

The Somerset skipper did say his team could walk out of Lord's with a lot of pride. What he didn't say was where they were walking to when the dew was well settled and the floodlights of Lord's had been switched off.

In a dimly lit London corner Marcus ordered an expensive round of Jägermeister as a big thank you to his team's efforts over the season. And that was just for starters, the beginnings of what by the night's end would exceed two grand from his pocket. The Somerset team, together with their small entourage, were in a nightclub whose bouncers Compo Dog – Zum's top scorer earlier in the day – had acquainted himself during his spell at Middlesex and through whom he'd managed to wangle both tickets and tables.

Happily one can chronicle that in the pervading gloom Somerset discovered the healing powers of laughter. Close in the nightclub's VIP lounge rapper Tinchy Stryder and the R&B singer Taio Cruz each wore a pair of dark designer shades. The music phenomena held court to an entourage of possibly nigh on a hundred glamour chicks.

The sight caused one waggish West Countryman to reduced his cricketing teammates into a fits of mirth by loudly posing the question: 'Hey mates, where's the bloomin' sunshine?'

* * *

In cricketing parlance, the word tragic can be overused. That didn't apply in Somerset. Around the County's towns and villages it felt more like an understatement.

Well after dawn broke on Sunday morning, and perhaps startled from a Wurzel tree, a blackbird chack-chack-chacked as the bronze impacts of Wiveliscombe church bells bim-bommed. But few folk finally returned from St. John's Wood wanting to pray to the Lord. The guddlers had simply drunk their sorrows into insensibility. Not a soul felt any anger with the Somerset team. And surely that was the reality across the length and breadth of the county. If anything, the devotion felt to its cricketers had risen full to popping.

For my part, I read Vic Marks' thoughts on the Championship in the *Observer*.

They were few and simple. 'The delicious agony of waiting continues in the West Country.'

* * *

Tucked away, there were two small appendices to the season. Mike Munday, his form in tatters, was, like Mark Turner, released. Perhaps he had had too many distractions. Like, for instance, a gossiped about late night encounter that arose when a shower of Somerset players had been knocking back vodka and rum in a not very salubrious Taunton nightclub.

A twenty-something squaddie – an Afghanistan veteran – with two girls in tow, separated himself from his mates and introduced himself at the bar. At kicking out time three players, Mike amongst them, had had been joined by the couple of 'young ladies'.

Woozy in the night air, the group hailed taxis home – a non-smoking shared flat provided by the cricket club. Mike was surprised when he got into his cab that the squaddie had hopped in, too. Asked what the hell he was doing, the squaddie pointed at the curvaceous figure beside Mike and said: 'that's my girlfriend.'

'Oh,' said Mike taken aback; and not being very big added chivalrously: 'you'd better come as well.' The Afghan vet received an indelicate high-heeled toe punt on his shin.

The laddish bragging started as the squaddie tried lighting a fag in the toaster. Told one had to be fit to have 'played for England under-19s' the squaddie fell to the floor and effortlessly did twenty one-arm press-ups. 'Can you do that?' he asked.

The reply from an anonymous player was instantaneous, and I paraphrase: 'don't be daft. We're cricketers, you numpty.'

Across the border in Devon the batting purist Mark Lathwell had called time on his cricketing career altogether, choosing instead the mysterious world of finance. Since leaving Somerset with two years left on his contract Mark had coached and captained Braunton, earning plaudits for what he had put back into the game's grass roots. Asked why Trough had finally given up club captain Jon Baglow quipped: 'I think he has found it frustrating this season not to score as many runs as he had hoped and seen players going out to have a slog getting more than him.'

SEVENTEEN

Calypso and Bunkers

'I've seen Labradors with more responsible tails.'

Anon.

It was in the bag. Well, Marcus Trescothick's driver was, along with various other weapons of mass destruction. 'I can give it a smash,' he said. A member at Enmore Park Golf Club within the sleepy Quantock Hills Marcus, playing off a six, had become very attached to his three wood, irons and wedges.

Indeed, he loved golf so much that in the wake of England's 2005 Ashes triumph he bought a luxury house on the undulating, leafy green Royal Westmoreland golf complex with ocean views. Logically, this sounds like it was north of Frome. It wasn't. Especially when one throws in diving pelicans, scruffy egret nests amidst acacia thorns, and lubricating *Carib*. Marcus' acquisition sat in Barbados. Due to his unfortunate flying phobia he'd never set foot in it, which is a pity because by reliable account there was a little rum shack on the course that apparently offered the best bacon sandwiches in the world.

However, the perfect opportunity for him to nosh one of these did present itself.

'We got invited out to the West Indies along with Hampshire in January 2011,' said Andy Hurry. 'We accepted, and went out there. As a club and as players we learnt a huge lesson: how to play on slow pitches where the ball sticks in.' He appeared to cringe inwardly. I didn't feel the need to ask whether there had also been a long lesson in how not to run between the wickets. On that particular subject I erred on discretion.

By finishing as runners-up in the 2010 Friends Provident t20, Somerset should have qualified for the 2010 Champions League Twenty20 but no English county sides were allowed to take part due to a clash with the end of the domestic season. So both Somerset and winners Hampshire were invited to escape the miserable English winter for some calypso cricket on islands where goats and chickens roamed and pitches were stony or, indeed, sandy. And incongruous to images of paradise, flowers of poinciana poked their heads prettily out of rust holes in vine entangled car wrecks. Wrecks of all sizes and makes rotted in front gardens and in the backs, and on every available patch of waste ground. Their seat foam kids found improvised as great cricket padding to go with bats made from coconut palms.

Here, the English sides were to compete in the 2010/11 Caribbean Twenty20. Somerset had every intention to make amends for the dejection and disappointment of not having won a domestic trophy the previous summer.

'You've got to learn how to win any competition,' Brian Rose told *BBC Points West*. 'If we can go out and win this competition it'll be a start for the year 2011. One or two have questioned what we're going to do to follow last year. All we can do is try and win something.' Famous last words.

The opposition was tough. Hampshire apart, pitted against Zum were Barbados, Jamaica, Leeward Islands, Trinidad & Tobago, Windward Islands, Combined Campuses & Colleges, and defending champions Guyana. The tournament's early rounds took place in Antigua. Barbados hosted the latter stages.

Encouragingly, Zum were able to call on the vast majority of their squad despite some diversions. James Hildreth, for instance, had been newly-appointed captain of England Lions. Another intriguing selection was Calum Haggett. The 20-year-old tall all-rounder from Shapwick, whom the club paid to attend Millfield School sixth form, was lucky to be alive. While playing for England Under-19s a routine check-up by the England team discovered he had a severe heart problem. Only by him being a professional sportsman was the trouble picked up. Now Calum, open-heart surgery for aortic root dilatation and a leaky valve behind him, had battled back.

Also included in the squad was Gemaal Hussain. Discovered in club cricket by Jack Russell, he had been training with Pakistan's national side. He, Steve Kirby and George Dockrell had a heaven-sent opportunity to start gelling into what Zum did as a squad.

And Nick Compton was brought back from Africa. He had made so many runs for Mashonaland Eagles that winter that there has been speculation he would be asked to represent Mugabe's twitchy Zimbabwe. Despite his mother being born in the country, Bob Marley singing 'Mash it up in-a (Zimbabwe) / Natty trash it in-a (Zimbabwe)' wasn't really Compo's thing. He wisely pledged his commit-

ment to Somerset and, he hoped, England.

Asked whether Marcus would be making the trip, chief executive Richard Gould told BBC Somerset: 'Marcus won't be going. That's definite.' Without hesitation, the lure of a bacon sandwich and a mystery house had been spurned. For him, any tour was out.

Hobnob, too, was absent. England demanded him in Oz. And Lewis Gregory was off to Sri Lanka skippering England Under-19s.

In the end, and with Alfonso Thomas elevated to captain, seventeen players and three backroom staff boarded the plane loaded with bulging kit bags. Gould wanted to avoid anyone being what he called 'home alone'. He would join the team after a week, as would Andy Hurry, who was in the Antipodes assisting with the England development squad.

Somerset's first match was against Guyana on a spanking new state-of-the-art ground, many people called 'Antigua's 366th beach', the local joke due to the sandpit of an outfield. A Test match begun against England on 13 February 2009 was abandoned after only ten balls due to the outfield's 'dangerous condition'. Financed with a Chinese Government grant, the cricketing venue, built on old sugar canes fields and prone to flooding, was actually called the Sir Vivian Richards Stadium. It encompassed underground passageways so that cricket teams could move around like Zum moles in their wontwiggles.

And to think Somerset's West Indian hero had but a pair of gates named in his honour at the County Ground.

Anyway, Guyana elected to have a bat, and Craig Meschede and Calum proudly made their Somerset t20 debuts. From a Zum perspective things seemed to be going hunky dory in first half of the game. Only a couple of Guyana's batters scored double figures and their tea, strangled for runs, limped to just 112 for 8 from their allotted 20 overs. At 51 for 5 Guyana looked in grave trouble but a 36-run partnership between Sarwan and Crandon inched them towards the 100-run mark after Suppiah went for 13 runs off one over. Captain Alfonso nipped out 3 for 23.

Somerset then cruised to 105 for 3 off 18 overs before they were stuck by what can only be called 'Headless Chicken Syndrome'. Suffering daft four run-outs, which were more of a case of swipe and pelt than tip and run, Somerset's demise was nothing other than calamitous. As a result of some tight Guyana bowling and electric fielding seven wickets clattered, four of them in the final over, for just 6 runs in thirteen balls meaning Zum lost by a paltry single.

Compo Dog, a sole boundary four to his name but well set on 32, had his stumps pranged first ball of the last over. Cor blimey, it seemed to have the same star-

tling effect in the Zum dressing room as a fox in a hen house. It was perhaps best someone tore the scorecard from the scorebook and gave it to a passing pelican to eat. Although the stadium may once have been a sugar-cane field there was nothing to sweeten the blow of such a shattering defeat. However, there were no new reports of flooding although Zum had quietly wept a tsunami of tears beside the sands. Capsizing all out for 'Nelson' was somehow appropriate given that the English seafaring hero had an unhappy stint on the island.

Somerset innings v. Guyana
(target: 113 runs from 20 overs)

		R	B	4s	6s
PD Trego	b Permaul	16	16	3	0
NRD Compton	b Crandon	32	47	1	0
JC Hildreth	c †Christian b Barnwell	5	13	0	0
JC Buttler†	c Crandon b Barnwell	18	16	1	1
AV Suppiah	lbw b Permaul	26	21	2	1
CAJ Meschede	run out (Crandon/†Christian)	1	3	0	0
AC Thomas*	run out (Sarwan)	0	0	0	0
CJ Haggett	run out (†Christian)	1	1	0	0
GM Hussain	run out (Dowlin)	0	1	0	0
SP Kirby	c Dowlin b Crandon	2	2	0	0
GH Dockrell	not out	0	1	0	0
Extras	(b 4, lb 2, w 3, nb 1)	10			
Total	(all out; 20 overs)	111			

Fall of wickets
1-23 (Trego, 4.1 ov), 2-32 (Hildreth, 7.2 ov), 3-62 (Buttler, 11.5 ov), 4-105 (Suppiah, 17.5 ov), 5-108 (Meschede, 18.4 ov), 6-108 (Thomas, 18.6 ov), 7-108 (Compton, 19.1 ov), 8-108 (Hussain, 19.2 ov), 9-111 (Kirby, 19.5 ov), 10-111 (Haggett, 19.6 ov)

Somerset's second match, and their consecutive game in the Sir Vivian Richards Stadium, was against the Windward Islands. This was altogether a much more successful affair. A sound allround bowling performance and no batting hiccups led to a comfortable 17-run victory. Oh, wonderfulness.

Winning the toss Zum chose to bat but lost their openers Arul Suppiah and Nick Compton within the first seven overs. James Hildrith and Jos Buttler put on 40 runs for the third wicket to steady the innings. Jos, who top-scored with 47, then combined with Craig Meschede to add 43 runs for the fourth wicket to take Somerset past the 100-run mark. Meschade and Alfonso Thomas hit some expansive shots as Somerset reached 139 for 4 off their 20 overs.

Windward's chase started poorly as Gemaal Hussain struck twice with his medium pace. Max Waller then picked up three crucial wickets with his leg-spin, including that of opener Johnson Charles, who top scored with 36. And that in truth was just about that. Suddenly, Zum were chipper.

Next stop Barbados. Against Jamaica, the contest, severely rain affected, was reduced to 6 overs a side at the Kensington Oval. Hurry, Gould and Taunton MP Jeremy Browne, on the island in his capacity as a Foreign Office minister, watched in disbelief. Somerset got a tousing.

Their only successes were winning the toss and Max Waller taking a sole wicket. Asked by Captain Alfonso to bat first Jamaica promoted Marlon Samuels to open. It was a decision that paid rich dividends as he dispatched Zum's bowlers all over the park as the basics of length and line disappeared out the window.

Together with Danza Hyatt the pair blasted 47 runs in three overs, including 14 runs off the first over bowled by Captain Alfonso. Though Hyatt fell for a breezy nine-ball 21 in the fourth over to Max, Samuels didn't let the momentum shift. He clubbed four fours and three sixes in his unbeaten 21-ball 45 and was particularly severe on Steve Kirby, whose only over went for 21 runs. And Jamaica reached an imposing 85 for 1 off their half dozen overs.

Faced with a daunting chase Zum capitulated with the willow. Jos Buttler went in the first over and after that it became procession. With four overs done and dusted Somerset were tottering at 17 for 6. They finally concluded at 24 for 8. It was an abject surrender. No Zum batter managed to reach double figures, and Calum Haggett had just played his last game in Somerset colours.

Jamaica joined the Windward Islands and Guyana at the top of the table in Group B. Zum had little to play for save pride.

With no realistic chance of qualification and the pressure off Zum faired better in their final game. James Hildreth top scored with 69, Nick Compton 44, and Craig Meschede weighed in with an 11 ball 26 as Somerset scored a healthy 165 for 4. In reply Combined Campuses and Colleges came up 42 runs short largely due to Steve Kirby taking 3-26 over which he was fist-pumpingly happy.

In a couple of months he'd be making a fresh season start in Blighty. But at least, as Andy Hurry said, Kirbs and his team-mates had learned the principals of how to play spin where the ball sticks in sandpits and bunkers.

EIGHTEEN

Lucky Hat and Splinters

'The art of being wise is the art of knowing what to overlook.'
William James, American philosopher (1842-1910).

Wearing his lucky beanie hat Baz is an odd-job man still leading a simple life grubbing around for acorns in the Quantock woods to sell by the bag to tree nurseries and having a daily flutter on whatever caught the eye at his local betting shop.

While not known to have a great knowledge of cricket, on the morning of 14th April 2011 and true to form he placed his money. And very pleased with himself he'd looked, too, once he'd done it. 'Bookmakers are a breed apart,' Baz had said.

Perhaps they had put the Caribbean calamities down to the impetuosity of youthful inexperience, or perhaps they weren't even looking, for the bookies had seemingly cast their minds back to the previous year and nodded in agreement. Somerset were their favourites to win the County Championship.

To assist in the gamble Zum put faith in the player nicknamed by Sri Lanka's TV pundits as 'Mysterious Bowler'. Balapuwaduge Ajantha Winslo Mendis had arrived with his suitcases, kitbag, scarf and fleecy gloves in time for the early season jousts. His inaugural taste of championship cricket came at Taunton under cloudy skies and in temperatures a tad cooler than Columbo. The opposition were a package of well wrapped Bears. Marcus Trescothick asked them to bat on an apple-green pitch which looked sure to assist the Zum seamers. Not a decision to benefit Mendis.

By the close of the first day Warwickshire had a total of 416 for six, and Richard Latham of the *Guardian* felt moved to tap the words: '"mystery spinner" had something of a nightmare.'

After being introduced into the attack which looked distinctly ordinary, and with Warwickshire 89 for one, Mendis conceded 124 runs from 24 overs, bowled in several spells, none of them displaying the control of line and length for which he was renowned. The only mystery was how he overstepped the line so often, sending down 12 no-balls off a run-up of no more than eight paces. Not only did these add to Warwickshire's total, they also chipped away at the bowler's fragile confidence.

The Warwickshire opener Varun 'Tidz' Chopra, the chief beneficiary of numerous Mendis long-hops, whacked a century. On the second morning the 'Bat of Barking' continued from where he'd left off and passed his double ton before Mendis finally got his man ell bee. However, Chris Woakes caused further Zum misery by hitting a hundred in as many balls before Warwickshire's run-fest concluded, all out for 642. In reply Somerset at the close of day two were 146 for 6, largely down to 62 from Arul Suppiah.

The cold light of day three brought carnage. All out in their first innings for 210, Zum were asked nicely by Jim Troughton to follow on. Woakes and Clarke went through them like a dose of salts. Shot out for a paltry 50 – of which Hobnob and Jos Buttler shared half – in a mere 14.4 overs constituted their lowest score since being bowled out for just 40 by Glamorgan at Swansea in 1968.

And, to add to the gobsmaking shock of it happening on Somerset's fabled run-laden Taunton track, it proved to be the third lowest total at the County Ground, Zum's second largest defeat and their heaviest since 1895. For the Bears it was their biggest win in their 117-year County Championship history. Holy moly, the Bears had dealt out a thumping by an innings and 382 runs.

Baz just smiled and tapped the side of his nose with his index finger, knowingly.

Social networking platforms, though, suddenly became rather active. 'Over the moon as a Bear ... but what was going on Somerset?' questioned Shakespear-esleftfoot. 'Bowled out at TAUNTON in 14 overs? That's madness, our attack isn't exactly Holding , Marshall, Garner and Roberts!'

One reply wasn't exactly chivalrous. 'I don my cap to you BEARS that you can even turn a computer on, let alone type a message to a website. Are your paws not to big?'

Another was prematurely fatalistic. "Shocking!! We are favourites now ... for the drop!!!'

Someone, in likelihood from across the Bristol Channel, had a retribution in mind inspired by grotty goings-on elsewhere in the world. 'If Glamorgan ever succumb to Rikki Clarke in that manner (offering 5 wickets for 10 in 3.4 overs) I'd personally brick the team bus! And dammit if they haven't got a bus I'd buy them one, herd the team onto it and then brick it.' Very droll. The month before, and enraged by Bangladesh's collapse to 58 all out and a thrashing, furious fans had hurled stones at the West Indies team bus – only for Imtiaz Ahmed, Dhaka's deputy commissioner of police to claim the mob meant to attack the home team instead. West Indies captain Chris Gayle tweeted at the time: 'Bangladesh stoning our bus!!! Freaking glass break!!! What next, bullets? This is ridiculous!!! I'm not keen here!' Thankfully, no one was hurt.

Happily for Zum's cricketers the Welsh lead wasn't followed. However, the inadvertent sound of splintering glass was, indeed, soon heard a couple of weeks later. The occasion? A rain affected CB40 game at Taunton against a Glamorgan Dragons side skippered by Alviro Peterson.

Despite the early loss of Trescothick, Trego had stayed put at the crease for about an hour and a quarter ploughing on to reach a hundred. He faced 58 balls with 8 fours and 6 sixes. One of those maximums came off Robert Croft when Tregs, having been going along nicely with Kieswetter, decided to 'kick on' and made such a mess that he became an overnight celebrity.

71-year old Edward Bevan of BBC Wales, on mike in the infamous potting shed he named 'probably the worst commentary box in the country', described the moment of impact. 'Robert Croft comes in now and bowls. And Trego comes down and hits it up towards us. And is it going to hit us?' The sound effect of splintering glass, a huge crowd cheer and then microphone muffle left one in doubt as to the answer. 'Sorry about that, Edward's had a blow in the back, I'm afraid.' said David James, Edward's fellow commentator, taking over the microphone and feigning nonchalance as though he'd come under fire in Baghdad. 'The ball has just come right through our window here.'

Edward he had lost the flight of the ball 'for a moment'.

Amidst shards of shattered glass Edward cowered shaken, a bruise purpling. Instinct had told him to turn away at the last second to prevent being hit in the face.

'Had I stayed where I was the consequences would have been much worse," he later admitted, having regained his composure. 'But I couldn't carry on. Dear old Steve James carried on for about a quarter of an hour.

'Apparently when the ball went through the window, Trego put his fist through the air as if to say "I've been trying to do that for years and I've done it at last"!

Everybody thought it was hilarious.'

Indeed, so much so that the morning after Somerset had ended up victorious and on their passage to another CB40 final Tregs, besieged by text messages, was delighted to feature on BBC Radio Two's Chris Evans Show as it, too, relived the instant of destruction.

'It was a bit of a comedy cartoon glass smashing sound – maybe I should have got ten runs. It's always nice when you can cause a bit of carnage – car windscreens are a favourite. It certainly means you're getting the runs,' quipped the tattooed vandal before sending his apologies to Edward.

As for the rain, it never seemed to stop. Although, when it briefly did all-rounder Roelof van der Merwe, signed for the first half of Zum's Friends Life t20 campaign to fill in for Pollard on Windies duty, proved outstanding in June's early group games. However, the bad weather had set in again when Hampshire Royals sloshed up at the County Ground mid week for their t20 engagement. Indeed, it fairly plothered down. This wasn't good. Dominic Cork's load of hogs had earned the reputation of being a pretty wild bunch and not ones for quietly lounging around with iPods, snoozing through DVDs or playing the likes of polka and whist.

With mallards paddling in the outfield play was abandoned without a ball being bowled. Liberated hogs sallied forth for a wet night on the Taunton tiles. Not finding much in the way of entertainment they decided to create their own by using the 'resources' available to them.

Their anonymous ringleader had the jolly wheeze of 'Grab a Granny' meaning that they should all try to 'get off ' with, and I hesitate to say this, ladies of more mature years. The rules were simple. The chap taken home by the oldest woman, and able to have his way with her, won. Simple. Most of the Hants lads were up for the challenge.

However, in a rumour that spread like wildfire, the jape backfired on one of their number. An upper order batsman, unwittingly described by Shaun Udal on Sky Sports as 'the finished article, polished in everything he does,' and 'class person-ified,' yet who shall remain nameless, found himself locked inside the house of a desperate housewife.

The unfortunate cricketer only managed to escape lascivious clutches by squirm-ing through the bathroom window. At two o'clock in the early hours he wandered Taunton quiet puddled streets dressed only in a towel, and completely lost. One could wonder if his red face came from a winner's glow of pride.

Sniggers about the affair still emanated from the Zum dressing room even when

Gloucestershire coach John Bracewell deposited his team upon Taunton's damp but drying sward in July whilst dangling a carrot – bragging rights. Having enjoyed success a week before in their Bristol 'sandpit', back-to-back t20 wins by the Shire over Zum were a modern rarity.

Both sides boasted a Murali. The Shire's was the non-drinker who confessed to know little about cider other that it 'encouraged noise'.

The Taunton after-workers began drifting in silently with the mizzle and were joined by a smattering of folk from up the M5 arriving incognito.

The locals looked apprehensively skywards and muttered about a badly draining outfield. There was no reason, however, not to drain the bar; adding to the urban myth that Twenty20 attracted football-like crowds whose intention it was to guddle as much as humanely possible within two hours.

Towards the tail of the queue came chunterings of calamity. Still with almost half an hour until the first was to be bowled in anger an administrative error or tragic oversight led me jotting a note into my black Moleskine notebook: '5.05. Cider's run out. Should have ordered double.'

Those from the Shire would have to adapt, as would their team to a Taunton playing surface that was the inverse of Bristol's. Yes, the wicket was great. Shame about the previous winter's newly laid outfield. As surfaces go it resembled a brand of expensively furrowed potato crisps. Throughout the season so far many a fielder had been in dismay, and derided of his teammates, as the ball bobbled through his legs after hitting the wrong end of a rut.

There was little of cheer. Not even fancy dress. I put it down to the Taunton crowd rushing straight from work. No time to become auk or elf, fluffy fresian cow or designer-stubbled nun. The proud owners of cardboard gladiatorial helmets wisely left them back up the M5 for fear of them getting soggy. There were, however, the Zum abundance of flimsy yellow plastic hard hats upon the heads of young and old – a marketing gimmick highlighting the destructive potential of captain Marcus Trescothick's merry band of tonkers.

Out on the field it was time for the players to maybe begin their warm-up on the announcement that Kane Williamson had won the toss and would 'have a bowl'. The only sensible decision given the clouds

At the far side of the ground from where I mingled with Goose and Mona, a couple of old friends from the Shire, Zum took the field not with practice bats but with a football, and began to show off their skills to spectators filling the Marcus Trescothick and Sir Ian Botham stands. Wearing a yellow bib, Peter Trego began to dribble.

Gazing out across the field, some cautionary words of former India captain and Zum opener until Gavaskar came to back me: 'Somebody should tell them nobody from Manchester United, Arsenal and Liverpool has come to scout talent here.' One of Sunny's top gripes was cricketers injuring themselves playing other sports during practice.

No such danger from the Shire boys. They were mostly huddled in the dug out, with the odd exceptions. Muttiah was nowhere to be seen.

Because of his Medici curls Hamish Marshall was easy to identify, not so with the rest of the team. Yes, names and numbers where on back of shirts but not on the back of their sweaters. Lanky quickie David Payne, however, did stand out. With him, perhaps more than Muttiah, rested the Shire's chalice of hope. The previous year, his 7 for 29 against Essex at Chelmsford was pretty damned decent. Just as Zum put their football away he began limbering and a'loosening.

Turning his left-arm over purposefully for real, Payne caused the flibberty jibbits.

Trescothick out, off stump uprooted second ball for a duck. Cue a pregnant pause of deathly silence, loudly broken by Goose. 'Ha ha ha!'

This was unfortunate. Mona gave Goose an almighty shove. 'Gawd's sake, wind yer neck in!' But she was too late. Needled into cussedness, Zum dug deep to preserve their vaulted reputation. By the interval between innings they had set a challenging total of 170.

In reply Marshall and O'Brien gave the Shire's chase a rollicking start by giving it some humpty.

Dear old Kirby got the run around, and it wasn't graceful. Arms pumping, body straining, he chased leather busting a gut. Whenever he managed to haul up the ball Goose and Mona, with the full force their lungs, shouted 'GLAWSTER-RRRRR!'

The glares Kirby sent their way were received with good humour and with relish. 'You wouldn't think Kirbs' such a pussy cat off the field,' chuckled Goose.

I had to smile, too, remembering Sky pundit Mark Butcher's remark: 'On the pitch Kirby goes a bit mad.' That was an understatement for such gold dust. Giving up a benefit to go and play for Zum, and never likely to get a full England cap, he gave his new club a hundred per cent. And why change a habit? He'd done exactly the same for the Shire, Old Bristolians, and Yorkshire before that.

Slowly the spirits of Goose and Mona began to ebb. The Zum bowlers chipped away, catches were held, and the run rate choked. In the battle of the Muralies,

Kartik, won the day. For the Shire there was no double as they slipped to a 15-run defeat. Zum supporters began to ensure their diaries would remain uncluttered for t20 finals day.

A week after the Shire game Zum welcomed India for the tourists' only warm-up match ahead of the season's Test series. And there were greetings anew in the home changing room. England captain Andrew Strauss had materialized like a cuckoo in desperate search of form after scoring just 27 runs in the Test series against Sri Lanka and two in his sole appearance for Middlesex against Gloucestershire, lasting just four balls before being ell bee to Jon Lewis. Perhaps with a maroon Zum helmet on his noggin and a true Taunton pitch he'd come good. It proved a vindicated gamble as he flayed a lacklustre visiting attack.

'They will be demanding a stand to be named after him at Taunton to join those celebrating Sir Ian Botham, Marcus Trescothick and Andy Caddick after this,' wrote Paul Newman in the *Daily Mail*. 'Andrew Strauss will always be an honorary Somerset man now.'

In his first innings he hit 78, sharing an opening stand of 101 with Arul Suppiah who went on to make 156. However, Strauss' knock that could easily have been cut short. When on 20 he looked desperately close to being ell bee to Zaheer but umpire Graham Lloyd, son of Bumble, shook his canny head.

Second time around he made hay, scoring a flawless unbeaten century – mission accomplished, as the full house that gave him a standing ovation testified. Andy Hurry summed up affairs. 'It was important that we gave it our best shot and really put them under the pump. We won the toss on a great batting pitch, dominated the game and started to bully them, which is a great position for England to sit back in their seats and appreciate what we have done for them.'

Reserving praise for Strauss, Sarge called him 'a real good egg', adding: 'He has an aura about him. The guys were listening to everything he said about batting and the England set-up. It's been positive from all sides.'

After tea on the third day, as clouds rolled in over the Quantock Hills and seagulls everywhere, proceedings came to a close. The result was a draw. Phillius, ever more confident of Somerset's t20 chances, felt waggish. Cupping his hands to his mouth he bellowed at the Indian players: 'Zum'll see you again in September in India!'

'Bloomin' 'eck, chap,' I said, 'first things first.' At the time it never occurred to me that this would mean an Edgbaston semi-final super-over eliminator. And blow me down it would be against those perishing custard coloured hogs, again. Putting it bluntly, Shahid Afridi did his level best to ruin Zum's travel plans on a day of rain, rain, and more rain during which, to the casual observer, Duckworth–

Lewis formulations became as complicated as quantum physics.

I had it on the Sarge's authority that the Somerset players had arrived at the newly redeveloped 'Bear pit' really relaxed with nothing other than their individual preparation to think about. He on the other hand had woken on the finals day morning finding it very hard to eat the hotel breakfast. But that apparently was part of his process of becoming ready. 'We've always played the second semi-final later on in the afternoon,' he said. 'We have a lot of time before we as a team travel to the ground. I go to the gym and get rid of a lot of nervous energy. And then I think about the game all the time. I usually get to the ground well before the players do.

'When I get there and see the atmosphere all of a sudden I go from uncontrolled to switched on. Now I've got my game face on as I meet the umpires and match officials.' Of the different things discussed that day at Edgbaston was what the Met Office had called 'a percentage chance of precipitation'.

Hampshire's innings was reduced to 15.5 overs. Afridi tonked 80 before a further deluge meant Somerset's target was 95 runs in 10 overs. Not a very generous equation.

Trescothick and Kieswetter, though, got off to a flyer. However, over by over the hogs' bowlers squeezed the run chase, wickets fell, and Zum were left needing one run from the last ball with Arul Suppiah on strike. Captain Cork resorted to gamesmanship, bringing himself and all the other fielders inside the circle. Short leg was so close to Arul that he could have tickled him. Determined, Arul heaved away only to find James Vince doing the honours of running Arul out. Thus the scores were tied. India was on hold, but in touching distance. For both teams the super-over was last chance saloon.

Somerset batted first. Afridi bowled. Between them Kieswetter and Buttler whacked 16 off the six balls. Now, with ball in hand, it was down to the Great Alfonso.

Afridi's magic touch deserted him. Two dot balls emerged from the first two deliveries. Afridi had merely wafted his willow at thin air. Third ball, an Afridi swipe connected. Four! Fourth delivery Arul bucketed a dolly. Afridi trudged back to the pavilion. Two balls later Hampshire had only managed an additional single. And that was that. Alfonso had become a hero. Hampshire's last-ball victory over Zum in the previous year's Twenty20 final was avenged.

'Super-overs – luck of the draw,' said Captain Cork matter-of-factly while Somerset once again celebrated a Champions League berth. 'Little' Leicestershire would be joining them by a squeak.

'By the most extraordinary coincidence both semi-finals ended in ties,' wrote Scyld Berry in the *Telegraph*. 'Never had a super-over eliminator been staged in county cricket before – and here were two in a day, to shred rain-soaked nerves.'

Surely, the pundits concurred, given the 'oppo', Trescothick's Somerset would at last lift a trophy. The cussed Foxes proved themselves to have had different ideas in a final that was relatively mundane. The most memorable moment being Paul Nixon's flying über-catch to dismiss both Polly and any lingering West Country hopes. Zum had been undone by the unassuming spin of Cobb and Henderson. The lessons learned in the Windies, temporarily at least, forgotten.

Sarge was philosophical. 'Every player understands they have a role to play within the side – a responsibility. If a player achieves it he should be proud of what he's done. But if he's let the team down that's a lot of emotional baggage to carry. As he walks off the pitch and comes into the changing room he's got to make sure he can offload and put it to bed before he goes out to the bench down the bottom. That's a very positive environment there, we can't accept anybody feeling sorry for themselves because they're other people going into bat and it has a huge emotional drain on them.' They were reasonable words in theory but, as Zum perpetually showed in pressure situations, they were jolly difficult to put into practice.

As September dawned promising its mists and fruitfulness the bookies had to admit Somerset had less chance of winning the Championship as a mealy-mouthed Exmoor pony had of winning the Grand National.

However, Baz still appeared upbeat as the Lancashire team coach pulled up in County Ground's car park prior to Zum's last Championship game of the season. The Great Alfonso standing for the crocked Trescothick became Captain Alf, won the toss and decided to bat. The top order wobbled. Young prospects Alex Barrow and Chris Jones went cheaply. The stage was set for James Hildreth to excel himself. When eventually caught off Tom Smith Hildy had mustered a knock of 186 that included 20 fours and a maximum. Unfortunately, Hildy's efforts weren't supported by the Somerset bowling attack, only Kartik with 6 for 127 caused any Lancastrian discomfort. And with both first innings completed the Red Rose county had a lead of a hundred having faced just 4 balls more.

Thereafter Zum were chasing tails and lost by 8 wickets. All was not well in the camp. Early on day three there had been a minor spat in the outfield between Tregs and Captain Alf. Something to do with field placements it sounded like. Hildy had illustrated how a cricketer's fortunes can rapidly change. He appeared to be dozing on the boundary when Kyle Hogg clipped the ball in the air towards him. Awoken by shouts of 'CAAAATCH" he took a few steps in, readied himself and then gaped as the ball plopped over his head, skipped inside the rope, and trickled for four.

'Switch on, buddy!' yelled the indefatigable Tregs.

Phillius also took umbrage, saying he would 'write to Mister Rose' and advise him to use 'a slipper and whacking stool.' More happily, Zum's second innings brought some light relief notwithstanding a clatter of wickets. Hogg had taken the scalps of Barrow and Jones and the Lancashire fast-medium was returning to his boundary post after completing an over. 'Tractor', arguably Zum's most loyal fan, waited patiently, bespoke tankard of cider in hand, to wind him up.

He succeeded.

'You want to look at the scoreboard – you're 30 for 3,' snapped Hogg, before heading off to bowl his next over. He conceded 14, mainly to a switched-on Hildy. Tractor scrutinized the bowler as he slouched back to the boundary.

Craning forward in an exaggerated effort to see the scoreboard, Tractor asked: 'What did you say the score was Kyle? We're looking for a good fast bowler down here for next season. Do you know any?' Hogg did nothing but glower. He needn't have because Lancashire cantered home. Despite Trego hooning a swing-and-hope day four rearguard 120, complimented by Kartik's 65 not out, the overall performance from a Somerset perspective was, in Phillius' words, 'piss poor'.

On the other hand, Lancashire had just crowned themselves County Champions.

Baz, to the amazement of all and sundry, began dancing a jig. 'It's because of my lucky hat,' he breathlessly explained to disapproving faces. What the rascal had gone and done at the beginning of the season was written abbreviations of each Division One county, bar Zum, with indelible thin black marker on individual acorns. These he'd dropped into his beanie. Having given that a shake and with his eyes closed he'd picked out an acorn. It happened to be marked 'Lanc'.

'I knew Somerset wouldn't win the thing. Went without saying,' he said, bouncing like a Tigger having cashed-in on enough for a 'good sesh' at his local.

Nil desperandum. Somerset's fourth place wasn't bad given the start they'd had. And Trescothick still had a chance of getting his mitts on some silverware. Zum had their CB40 final appointment with Surrey within 48 hours.

NINETEEN

Ambassadors and Surgical Dressings

'An ambassador is not simply an agent; he is also a spectacle.'
Walter Bagehot, journalist born in Langport, Somerset, (1826 –1877).

Dissimilar to the native Ambassador 'the king of Indian roads' since 1958, admittedly with few improvements or changes from its origin as a Morris Oxford, the bunch of country boys had returned as ambassadors of Somerset cricket after a two-year absence.

Cricket has a delightful habit of perverting the course of logic. It would have been a winsome delight if, after finishing runners-up in various competitions seven times in the past three domestic seasons, Zum had ended their search for a trophy by winning the Champions League. Always a bridesmaid, never a bride; 2011 was their chance to elope overseas.

It had all been a bit if a kerfuffle heightened by the deluge of flashes from hundreds of mobile phones and the hit of the Indian media as soon as Zum set foot off the plane. Although boosted by the return of left-arm spinner Roelof van der Merwe, the second overseas player alongside Murali Kartik in a potent spin attack, odds of 12-1 reflected the fact that they were without three of their best players: Trescothick, Kieswetter and Buttler – the latter two being available later in the tournament after England duty against the West Indies.

With Gemaal Hussain unable to get a visa, Chris Jones grasped his opportunity as depleted Zum steeled themselves to play Aukland Aces in their first Champions League qualifying match in Hyderabad. 78 hours earlier the County had put on an insipid display in the CB40 final at Lord's.

That match had proved an unmitigated disaster. Somerset having won the toss elected to bat despite the very real threat of rain influencing events. This appeared a bit muppety. Some in the ground suggested it accommodated the return from injury of Captain Marcus. Get him batting before further crocking was the cunning plan, they believed. If that was the reason it came to nowt. Zum lost their talisman skipper cheaply – a loss exacerbated by other major batters making grotty shot selections. Suddenly the team were in a hole larger than a Millfield rabbit's. Jos Buttler batted brilliantly to make 86 but Steve Kirby, finding himself all too soon at the other end, haplessly swung and missed for four or five balls an over.

Having just secured promotion from the Second Division of the Championship Chris Adams' Surrey had been totally 'up for it'. Their fielders were noisy as sparrows in a bush, their bowlers aggressive. Somerset, on the other hand, looked as motivated as chuggy pigs. Needless to say Surrey won easily.

Sarge allowed himself a smirk upon my mentioning sparrows in India being viewed as aphrodisiacs. Due to their public exhibitions of libido they had become a somewhat rare treat. My little avian fact gave him the opportunity to gloss over the Lord's debacle and switch tack to 'incredible results' in Hyderabad.

The game against Aukland Aces was a cliffhanger of the crumbly sort. Batting first the Kiwi side, given the pitch, hit a respectable 125 for 7. It became squeaky bum time as Somerset, having recovered 54 for four in 9.2 overs, found themselves on 124 for 5 with two balls of the last over of their innings remaining to be bowled. With the stadium holding its breath James Hildreth smoked Michael Bates through the covers. The ball was fielded in the deep by Munro. Hildy and Steve Snell pelted one and excitedly turned to steal a second. Alert, Munro fired a throw perfectly to the keeper. The bails were whipped off. Hildy was run out by a country mile.

It was down to Captain Alf. Déjà vu. Two years before, at the very same venue he had scored the winning runs. Now 1 run was needed off the final delivery. Full and wide outside off the Great Alfonso leant and managed to get it over cover. The batters crossed before the ball reaches the ropes. Somerset had won and surely shaken off the jet lag. Snell unbeaten on 34 off 24 balls was named Man of the Match.

It was a far cry from playing club cricket for Bristol and a bit for Hertfordshire in between coaching at Millfield School and commentating on Somerset's games for BBC radio.

'Snelly. What a story!' exclaimed Sarge. 'What a hero! Yet he may never play another game of professional cricket ever again in his whole life.' In Sarge's office, his and my conversation had moved to the little know cricketer released by Gloucestershire, and without a first-class contract, whose life had turned topsy-turvy from the moment Somerset had found themselves in the unusual position

of having both of their wicketkeeping options on England call up.

Sarge recalled the exploits of Steve Snell fondly. 'He started working so hard. So much positive energy. Picked for that first game Snelly said: "cor, I'm going to enjoy every single second of this, every second." But my God he was nervous.'

Of course, the story nearly didn't happen. The timing was atrocious. When Snelly got 'the call' in late August there was the small matter of him being in a hospital bed undergoing an operation on a putrid leg. Not that anybody had let on to Brian Rose, Zum's director of cricket, about that.

Snelly was Steve Kirby's idea when Zum were banging their heads as to whom the hell they could have behind the stumps and able to bat in Twenty20, too. Initially they toyed with the idea of fielding the teenage Alex Barrow. But, bless him, he was still at school and wasn't even the regular wicketkeeper for the second team.

So Kirbs had a word with Sarge who in turn whispered in Rosey's ear. 'Right,' said Rosey, 'let's go and have a look at him and put him down'.

Luckily for Snelly, because of the nature of the injury, there was no structural damage and it was not a muscle injury. There was just a gaping wound. Having got that patched up he didn't need Steve Kirby's powers of persuasion to drag him out of bed and to get his backside down to the County Ground for a fitness test to see if could actually play or not. It was a case of mind over matter.

Within days he helping Somerset into the CB40 semi-finals with victory over Essex. More than likely he wasn't in the least bit fit to play, but when such opportunities come along players have to grab them.

'I played with a huge smile on my face the whole game, because I never thought I was going to get this chance again,' Snelly admitted. 'I sent a text message to Geoff Twentyman from Radio Bristol before the Essex game, telling him I was playing and asking if he wanted me to interview myself after the game.'

An outing for a single day's Championship cricket was the only other chance of match preparation he had before hopping on the plane, grateful Somerset had secured him a visa from the Indian High Commission in London. Somerset had also overcome more red tape to receive a special dispensation to draft Snelly in from the Champions League organisers. 'I think we might have been made to look ridiculous had we not taken a specialist keeper,' Rosey said on the club's website.

On the morning the Aukland Aces game in the most prestigious tournament in 20-over cricket after the World Cup – the Champions League t20 Snelly was collared by Paul Radley of *The National* – an English-language daily newspaper published in Abu Dhabi. 'Playing in the Champions League in India is pretty much a fairytale story,'

said Snelly thoroughly looking forward to stepping out at Rajiv Gandhi Stadium to keep wicket though confessing: 'there is still a big wound which is still healing.'

'But now I'm here I want to go out and put in a couple of good performances to help Somerset qualify for the second phase. This is a massive shop window for me.' Indeed, it was especially as a day after the Aukland Aces game Zum were to play Kolkata Knight Riders. For Zum to qualify for the competition proper they had to do it the hard way.

There's nowt better to create scoreboard pressure than a good old weight of runs. Somerset attacked the KKR spin attack with an uninhibited mindset and waltzed to an imposing 166 for 6, with Pete Trego hitting 70 in 81 balls. KKR were listless in the field and then out-bowled being pushed to the brink of elimination. To prove it was their batsmen's skills and not the pitch that enabled the victory, Zum's spinners picked up 6 for 86 runs to beat Kolkata at their own game. Somerset had won by 11 runs. Tregs got Man of the Match. 'I'm proud, so proud,' he said, his eyes glistening in the post match interview. 'It's one the best days of my life.'

The match poised, turned on a moment of extraordinary brilliance from the dynamo that's Roelof van der Merwe. With the angle Bangladeshi Shakib Al Hasan played a pick-up pull off Trego, bulleting the ball well to the right of deep square. Roelof flew full length to his right to take it with both hands. 'You know 99 times out of 100 there's an opportunity for those to pop out,' said Sarge, animatedly. 'A game changing moment – the difference between staying in the competition or getting on a plane and going home. The belief kept growing and growing and growing.'

For their part the Indian side needed 153 to qualify for the CLT20 main draw, too. That they got them, finishing on 155 for 8, was purely down to an ice-cool Ryan ten Doeschate. With the tournament's group stage set and ready to go KKR would shortly meet Somerset again at the same venue.

After they had done so Abhishek Purohit was moved to write not about Roelof's fielding but his batting: 'At times, a batsman takes so much control over the flow of a game that even a partisan crowd is stunned into silent acceptance of an inevitable defeat. That moment arrived in the tenth over of Somerset's chase when Roelof van der Merwe, who had already brutalised his way to 62 off 30, got a bouncer from Jacques Kallis.

Van der Merwe's response was to arch back and guide it over the wicketkeeper. He ended up playing the shot so delicately that the ball went to the fine leg boundary. There was a gasp from the crowd as it realised decisively that Kolkata Knight Riders had run into a batsman so confident in his approach that there was no stopping him.'

Sarge simply described the South African as 'incredible'.

Coming into bat the first ball of the second over Roelof proceeded to dominate so much that Pete Trego managed only 23 out of a 105-run second-wicket stand. Even when KKR, through the guises of Kallis and Yusuf went berserk, Roelof was the only man to hold his own. He went for just 14 from the 18th and 20th overs despite two dropped catches, one of which went for four.

With the bat in hand he was an absolute jack in the box, reverse-sweeping sixes, managing to mishit over the infield, drop-kicking his favourite cricketer Kallis over midwicket, late-cutting the spinners delicately, and scoring the third-fastest Champions league fifty. When out caught and bowled by Shakib Al Hasan he had plundered 73 of 40 balls with 9 fours and 2 sixes.

Roelof later admitted that the knock was much more than his usual frenetic cameos. 'I felt that it was one of my more controlled innings upfront,' he said, aware of the active role he had to play at No.3 in the absence of Hobnob and Jos. He gave it everything.

Whatever KKR threw at him, the boundaries just kept coming. He played the late cut, he drove over cover, he whipped over midwicket. He even reverse-swept for six. That last shot brought a playful intervention from Captain Alf at the media briefing. 'Don't encourage him,' he told a reporter who queried Roelof how he had managed to play the shot. When a deft upper cut was mentioned, Roelof said with a straight face that he was 'just trying to get out of the way' of the ball.

They were cruising at one moment and it looked as if they will finish the game by the 16th over. But KKR bounced back, inflicting a couple of casualties on Zum in the 14th over. A couple of quick wickets after that and Zum were clearly trying to snatch defeat. Halfway through their final over they still needed 2 with Snelly at the non-striker's end. Rajat Bhatia produced a length delivery in the line of the sticks Compo Dog shuffled across the stumps and scooped it over short fine leg for a boundary. 'Wooooo' roared Compo as he punched the air. Somerset 2, Kolkata Knight Riders 0.

Somerset moved on to encounter the mighty Gale force atop the Royal Challengers Bangalore order. And Jos Buttler, back in the Zum starting eleven, could only hang his head in despair after a severe case of droppage. Chris Gale made room and, with a bat three times the size of Captain Alf's, had a go at a Kirbs full delivery to produce a steeper over extra cover. Jos seemed to have it covered in its meteoric descent over his shoulder. He laid two to hands to it but it was too hot to hold. Two runs were the outcome and the first couple towards the man mountain's 86 in a 46 ball blitzkrieg.

Chasing a mammoth 206 Somerset fell 51 runs short. The defeat meant they had to beat the South African outfit Warriors in Bangalore, typically the highest scoring venue of the tournament, to reach the semi-finals.

Somerset's 146 seemed a below-par effort that embraced the innings highlight –
a Jos monster hit over long-off which landed on the roof of the Chinnaswamy
Stadium. Kieswetter, who batted through the innings for his 56 that included 4
fours and 3 sixes, was really down on himself for not pushing the side to a bigger
score.

But with the attendant financial rewards, on the line, Captain Alf bowled a near-
perfect penultimate over to end South African hopes.

He began with a short ball that evaded Craig Thyssen outside off, and then had
Thyssen mowing a catch to deep midwicket. There was a single off an inside-
edge on the third ball and Wayne Parnell was then fooled by a slower delivery. An
almighty heave from a desperate Parnell ended up as a catch to wide long-on
before a leg-bye rounded off a two-run over, the least expensive one of the
innings.

Captain Alf's heroics left the Warriors needing a herculean 21 off the final six
deliveries, which proved beyond them. Somerset won by a dozen runs.

Full of praise for his side, Captain Alf singled out Zum's 20-year-old debutant,
Exeter born seamer Adam Dibble – 24 runs off four overs and a wicket. 'He's come
in for his first game, went for 13 in his first over and came back and probably
bowled one of the better spells of his life,' Captain Alf said. 'It just shows the character of this team. We came here, nobody gave us a chance, let's face it, but everybody has pulled together and that is exactly what this team is about.'

Somerset had become the first English side to make the semi-finals of the Champions League t20 and were off to Chennai, which in the words Captain Alf was
as 'hot as Hades'. Between Zum and a berth in the final stood the Mumbai Indians
and the hazards of 'Slinga Malinga' and, ironically, Keiron Pollard.

'There was no need for a warm-up,' reflected Captain Alf. 'After just walking off
the bus it wasn't long before I was wet through.'

Winning all the decisive moments of the night Mumbai chose a fine time to put
up their best batting effort of the tournament. Zum faced a Blizzard of runs in
more than hyperbole. After their 20 overs Mumbai were asking Zum to chase
down 160.

Reduced to 17 for 2 after three overs Somerset refused to capitulate. Both of
Somerset's tournament top scorers, Tregs and Roelof, 'Malingered'. But nil
desperandum. Hobnob was on fire.

Kieswetter played like a man who knew he would win the match if he took it
deep. Missed on 31 and 50, he began the acceleration. And on Jos Buttler coming

to the crease after the fall of Hildy's wicket 61 were left to score off 39.

However, with the runs needed down to 29 off three overs Malinga still had twelve balls left in his locker. His next over cost just seven. Was it all part of Zum's ploy? 'We had discussed a real tactic of damage limitation against him, knowing that we could capitalise on the lesser bowlers,' said Captain Alf.

So, against the left-arm of James Franklin in the 19th over, Jos, adrenaline pumped, gave it a dash.

The first ball was drilled wide of long-on. Only Pollard could have kept it from going for four. Being blooming professional, he did. Then came catastrophe. Jos butchered the next delivery, a full toss, straight back down the ground. Hobnob charging for the single was in no position to react and he became a deer caught in the headlights. The ball thudded sickeningly into his left forearm. Denied a sure boundary, Zum lost momentum. Jos lost his head. Maybe thinking he deserved eight off those two balls whereas he only got two, frustrated, he played a blind slog to the third ball of the over and was castled.

Hobnob managed to regain strike to the fifth. He had faced only six deliveries out of the previous 27. Now with 19 required off eight, six of which would be bowled by Malinga, he had no choice. Hugely restricted from the ill-fated blow he went after a short-of-a-length ball, and top-edged. Sods Law, Pollard, of all bods, was underneath it to snatch away the Somerset dream. In minutes they had demised by 10 runs and, bags packed, would fly home the following day. Just as well really because Snelly was due to get married and have his surgical dressing checked.

'It's been a seriously long journey and, I suppose, great that we got so far,' said Captain Alf. 'Everywhere we go cricket lovers run up holding out their phones in the hope of a photograph and signature. For any of us, this adoration and atten-tion is special. I thought I was doing well when I got a free Starbucks in Taunton after a good innings for Somerset, but this takes it to a new level. Playing against the likes of Brett Lee, Gayle, Jacques Kallis and just about every big name in cricket is awesome, and having the chance to rub shoulders with them and talk is even better.

'I cannot explain how fantastic the support has been for us: messages on Twitter and Facebook, and other opposing team coaches congratulating us on our attitude and heart. There's no doubt we all feel hugely proud to be here representing Somerset, and also England.'

On a final note, by Sarge's reckoning anyway, Somerset having reached the Cham-pions League semi-final made them a top four domestic cricket team in the world. Possibly.

TWENTY

Endpiece

'Same old slippers, Same old rice, Same old glimpse of paradise.'
Colonel William James Lampton (1859 – 1917).

Before Christmas Somerset decided to immortalize Brian Rose at the County Ground by naming a pretty wide pair of silvery gates opening onto the bankrupt Brewhouse Theatre in his honour.

Far away in India Nick 'Compo Dog' Compton slipped on his first England shirt. He and his England team-mates led by Alastair Cook had won two Tests and in so doing had achieved an historic series win. Billy the Trumpet played 'Jerusalem' among the draped flags of St. George. The Anglophiles, some in sunhats made from folded copies of *The Statesman* and the *Times of India*, were raucous. And the Barmy Army had even sung Compo's name.

'I'm not sure what the words were,' he joked, 'but the sound of Compton resonating around Eden Gardens was something I never thought would ever happen.' Questions of whether he belonged or was good enough to play with guys he'd watched and looked up to had gone through his mind.

Off the field of play, forty-minute training sessions overseen by Graham Gooch in the searing Indian heat had Compo Dog netting for six balls, sprinting back and forth weighed down with handmade bricks, netting a further over, followed up by ten burpees, something equally as silly to the constitution as squat thrusts. And then the whole shenanigans were repeated ad nauseam before he was allowed time off to get beaten at chess by orphan kids.

Back in Blighty the Summer Land had turned on its head. Cricketing preparation during the early spring of 2013 seemed as far removed from Compo Dog's in the Subcontinent as possible to envisage. There had been gossip of cricketers pole dancing. Captain Marcus was baking carrot cake and mint choc chip muffins for charity. Max Waller tweeted creepy coincidences between US president's Lincoln and JFK. And to top that past Zum heroes Biff and Punter had been signed by Surrey, an influential nab, it was said, by the former Zum, now the feather plume county's chief executive, Richard Gould.

Taunton Starbucks, though, had seen an upturn in morning trade with a return of the County's professionals. Not exactly in their salad days, Hildy sipped caffè Americano while 'The Great Alfonso' possibly deferred to swig 'take out' whole bean and a roll-up. Rather that than partake in the Somerset team's 7.30 am official breakfast regime consisting of bland baked fish accompanied by raw broccoli and carrots.

Sad to relate Zum's pre-season friendlies over Easter were equally underwhelming. Having given up the radiators for snow flurries Somerset found themselves well and truly diddled by a Hamish Marshall led Gloucester. Watched by Dave Nosworthy their lauded new director of cricket, Somerset were beaten by 104 runs. A few days later they became victims of Middlesex who dealt out a 9-wicket thrashing. 'The county championship's obviously a focus for us but I'm no magician – I'm not making any promises,' announced Dave, previously coach of the Canterbury Wizards.

Mind you, Zum weren't at full strength. Far from it.

By now Compo Dog was swanning around with England in New Zealand. And Steve Kirby and the chap of the asymmetrical tattoos journos had affectionately started to call 'T.R. Ego' were away in the United Arab Emirates as part of the MCC side being ground into the desert, and the ignominy of an innings defeat, by the county champions Warwickshire in Abu Dhabi's Sheikh Zayed Stadium. With Blighty's freezing weather it was a pity the two Somerset chaps couldn't help prolong the game if for no other reason than to sustain their own warmth.

But things weren't all bad. Indeed, Kirby scintillated on his return. And in the final warm-up game Division 1 new boys Derbyshire were annihilated by an innings and 30 runs. Zum were wise, though, not to get carried away at a change of fortune.

Up the Wellington road, however, the Welsh bison Steffan Jones was about to be. Set to continue his love affair with India, and the preferred choice to Craig McDermott, Steffan had a new feather in his cap. Flight and expenses paid he was bound for Rajasthan and its Jaipur cricket academy. 'I've been asked to be their fast bowling and cricketing consultant,' he proudly told me.

There was every chance I felt that in Steffan lay the future of Somerset cricket. Even the County's head coach one day, maybe. The Welsh bison certainly held such self-belief as he bade me farewell before disappearing from sight through the gurt double doors into the heart of Wellington School's Princess Royal Sports Complex. Had he the art of clairvoyance Jamie Cox once exhibited in his 2001 *Postcard*? Well, those of Somerset persuasion would have to wait and see.

Meanwhile, Margaret Thatcher the longest serving prime minister in 150 years was two days dead when Compo Dog was named one of *Wisden's* five cricketers of the year in its 150th edition, so emulating his grandad Denis who achieved the accolade in 1939. Much to Compo's pleasant surprise Denis had greeted him not that long beforehand. A faded black and white photograph of the 'old chap' at the crease hung on the changing room wall in Nagpur. 'Think his head is falling over,' quipped the grandson, now a rightful expert, at Denis' stance.

Nominated for his achievements in the previous English summer Compo was possibly further helped by scoring back-to-back Test match centuries in Kiwi Land – his maiden in Dunedin under the gaze of Geoffrey Boycott warbling on TMS about sticks of rhubarb and the second five days later in Wellington.

By the time the old Harrovian's name appeared on the Somerset team-sheet his team-mates had already pootled up to Durham to lose the first championship match of the infant season on a bitch of a pitch. Happily with his inclusion, albeit a rather unproductive one, Zum emerged with a draw against Surrey at the Oval thanks to debutant Alviro Peterson's masterly century. Biff's opening partner for South Africa had got off to a flying start.

The match highlight though came from the indomitable Trego. The tearaway of ten years ago had become a canny operator, a fine springtime bowler heading towards the autumn of his career. He bowled just two balls to Biff. The first was his regulation inswinger to the left-hander, tucked away for a single. The second possessed a lethal straightness. It found the outside edge of Biff's bat and Hildreth took a diving wonder catch at first slip. T.R. Ego did his best to look nonchalant.

So it wasn't until the end of April that Somerset had their first home game of the campaign. In an encounter billed worthy of telly, the 'Bear and Ragged Staff' rippled from the flagpole above the Caddy Shack's visitors' changing room. Umpires Saggers and Cook looked perished in the low-degree temperature. The cold wind from the Quantocks whistling through the mid-off gap between the Sir Ian Botham stand and the Colin Atkinson pavilion appeared to help drift as balls challenged the outside edge. The daily papers of brave spectators in mufflers and beanie hats cuddling thermoses rustled. Dogs, even a refined golden retriever sporting a Somerset club tie, shivered. Numb fingers clicked digital cameras, snapping up poses of Alviro Peterson clipping four after four or Craig Kieswetter punching the air as he got off nought with his new Millichamp and Hall made

in the old barn behind the cricket museum. Someone in the Caddy Shack it seemed had been gently winding Hobnob up.

As for Compo Dog, the bitter chill turned his nose crimson while on his merry way to a ton. He reached three figures by clattering a six-ball just below the nattering box windows. Bumble, Knight, Atherton and Hussain et al ducked instinctively out of pure self-preservation. Marcus declared 'enough'.

Moments later the big crusher was on to flatten the wicket. The Bears had four and a half sessions to survive. And this they did, but not without incident, including some broken bones.

'We always seem to meet at times like this with Somerset just failing to win,' smiled a chirpy Athers on Sunday evening Sky Sports duty having collared a brave faced Marcus for the obligatory post match interview. Somerset had come up a wicket shy of deservedly beating Warwickshire whose 427-9 was their highest second-innings total in first-class cricket. When their number eleven Hannon-Dalby bravely gritted his teeth and played a forward defensive to the final ball Zum's fielders remained in position, heads bowed in abject dejection. The gangly left-hander had survived 62 deliveries, half of them with a broken hand.

However, the draw was nothing but contentious. The Zum skipper, one of the greatest ball polishers in the world, had stood at first slip throughout the Bears second innings doing just that, and was perhaps left regretting his decision not to enforce the follow-on when the visitors were bowled out for 158. Bearded, young Jack Leach, still the owner of a smart blue second XI cap, snaffled a career best 'fifer' with his slow left-arm spin and ultimately Man of the Match. It meant the Bears were 248 runs short of Somerset's first innings effort of 406.

Admittedly, Zum did hinder themselves a tad. There were an irritating couple of dropped slip catches in not the best of light. Cor lummy, Hildy's was regulation. But with leather nearly removing his schnozzle, Alviro's was somewhat tougher. Both chances came off the Great Alfonso. His scowls of botheration darkened the heavens further. Rikki Clarke's luck was in. Hobnob's was out, nobbled after freakishly fracturing his thumb.

Yet, Somerset had given it everything. They had dominated the match. Ten out of ten for effort and passion. The massive teenage unit of Jamie Overton was out on his feet. But oh, how to a man his team-mates had prematurely joined him in celebration.

Bumble, patron of Accrington Cricket Club, spoke as a sage. 'Cricket can be a cruel, but that makes you a better person. Well, some say that.'

'We were robbed!' heckled a grizzled lingering spectator. The voice was that of

Phillius, well informed via his mobile what TV replays had repeatedly confirmed.

Marcus kept his own counsel but was entitled to cast a rueful glance at spectacled umpire Nick Cook, rosy cheeked possibly from embarrassment. Perhaps he'd been the only person at the County Ground not to have seen or heard last man Hannon-Dalby edge Jamie to Jos Buttler, who, having taken over Hobnob's duties pretty much as he'd done for England, took the 'catch' with gauntleted simplicity an hour before the scheduled close of play.

Having an awful match and his confidence low, Umpire Nick with the wide-eyed panic of uncertainty kept his index finger tucked away warm in his white coat pocket to deny a home win. The ironic sponsor's logo of a national chain of opticians on the Warwickshire shirts gave a hint as to where Mister Cook should be headed come the Monday morning.

So Zum had ended up with eleven rather than twenty-four points. How important would that difference be come the reckoning under autumn's clouds? Phillius must have caught my thoughts. 'Any more misfortunes and we'll be playing regular red ball cricket with blooming Gloucestershire again,' he lamented somewhat disparagingly toward the Shire languishing in Division Two.

To be blunt it seemed that Summerlanders would have to wait a bit longer for the chimera that is the County Championship. Another Somerset century was now in its thirteenth year and supporters of a nervous disposition were crossing their fingers. Others were alarmist about Somerset's prospects of the drop. 'They're already looking down the barrel,' piped Jonathan and Jason, the local butcher twins, fatalistically in sync.

To avert such catastrophe there was plenty of work to do and training to be done.

'You either get luck or you don't,' said Sarge. 'But you tend to give yourself more good luck by making sure you just keep working hard all the time because you've got more chance of being successful that way. And we've performed poorly in high profile final games. There's no doubt. It's the pressure associated to it. The pressure about us winning trophies gets more and more and more. It's expectation.' Too damn right.

The white ball t20 wham bam was almost over the horizon. On the walls of the 'Bearin' Up', the affectionate name for Wiveliscombe's *Bear Inn*, where old dog-eared fly-posters for snazzy Twenty20 'Hitty Hitty Bang Bang' vied for space with fresher affairs declaring 'Danger – Batsmen at Work' there was just room for 2013's 'THWACK' ad.

Before that, though, the usual fluffy extroverts had arrived for Zum's first YB40 game of the season. Grouped amongst the crowd were an acceptable goat, a pot-

belled yellow duck, a manky lion, and a rather decrepit fox. But the jury was out as to whether the sweaty, bearded bloke inside a white, black spotted costume was meant to be a Dalmatian, a peeled dragon fruit, or Stracciatella gelato ice cream.

A Zum fielder, tenaciously stood at point, rubbed his eyes. Not at the apparitions in the stands but at the risky scampers of Unicorns. More unexpectedly, one even nibbled at a passing leather sphere.

Just turned 40, Unicorns skipper Keith Parsons had materialized for the day from the fluorescently lit interior of the County Sports shop only to receive a third ball duck. As 'keeper Buttler and bowler Meschede celebrated between themselves Keith could only, tuck his bat under arm and trudge back to the visitors dressing room of his beloved County Ground and put his feet up.

For the more youthful, gossip revealed pole dancing to be the new fitness innovation designed for 2013. Hellfire, Sarge was still at it theorizing how to help with players' relaxation and flexibility.

The mind boggled at what attributes Somerset's cricketers would discover about themselves – and this on top of yoga's resurgence. Suppressing a giggle, things to me were beginning to smack of desperation in the attempts to create a team of thoroughbreds that in *Top Gear* parlance were the very essence of reliability but, of course, without the irritations of choke.

'We're really close, but we need to know how to get over the line,' Dave Nosworthy muttered unfazed. 'There's no exact answer. It will just take a bit of polishing.' Well, Hallelujah, I thought. A pole could have that effect.

To be fair Somerset try everything – the Marine camp, weight training, speed running, cycling – you name it. Somerset are big on training. Steffan Jones might take some credit for that. But there's only one main explanation of them being where they now are as a team and that is Justin Langer. Yes, the Taunton crowds got a bit fed up with him, but folk need to remember the reason why the County has become successful.

Also, the Somerset Academy, now one of the best in the country, has become a victim of its own success. Agreed, it provides some exceptional players for Zum, but then the cream pops off to England. The future though is bright. Faith will inevitably shift onto the likes of Leach, Meschede, Gregory and Dibble. And the wisecracks are just beginning about the batsman being Abell.

Under Captain Marcus, Somerset can but continue to strive for the cricketing silverware he and his cohorts crave and annually come so very close to achieving. For my part I've become weary of hearing Phillius and others Summerlanders

unsportingly swear their frustrations. So may the idiom 'always the bridesmaid never the bride' soon return to whence it was intended – as the marketing catch-phrase of *Listerine*.

* * *

On the 11th May, around the moment Wigan Athletic astonishingly won the FA Cup at Wembley, Lewis Gregory, skipping and juggling in front of and behind the Headingly boundary rope, wound-up with a catch of brilliance to bring defeat upon Yorkshire Vikings in the YB40 and somewhat poop their 150th Anniversary celebrations.

The White Rose kingdom had not just been turned over it had been dismantled and Bob Marley pulsing from the loudspeakers singing 'don't worry about a thing / 'Cause every little thing gonna to be alright', did little to soothe.

England's one-day wicky Jos Buttler was destroyer in chief. Staggeringly innovative, his power and the finesse of his little reverse paddles brought him 89 off 51 deliveries, smashed 10 fours and four sixes in a trademark blast. He hit the ball '360', and on one occasion larruped it so hard that it bounced into the old committee room – the haunt of Boycott, Close and hot words of argumentation.

Zum's 338 for 5 was the highest against Yorkshire at Headingly. Jos shared 129 in 14 overs for the fifth wicket with Hildy, who actually top-scored with 96 not out off 84 balls.

Everything Somerset did was ordered, structured, and well thought out. And winning by 131 runs meant it was their largest triumph against Yorkshire in the 40 over format of the game.

'Vikings pillaged, today,' Bob Willis had commented. And revenge for their invasion of Watchet in 977, I had thought to myself.

When writing anything about Somerset it's always difficult to know where to put the final full stop. As soon as the author feels inclined to do so events conspire to make him think 'dammit!' By concluding this tome here and now at least this special County is left in a state of slightly heightened optimism. Not least because little Yeovil Town had heroically got themselves promoted to football's Championship. Miracles happen. Suddenly sleepy Somerset was wide-awake.

I just hoped its professional cricketers could keep it that way as the season continued to unfold. All was still to play for with *The Blackbird* being lustily sung.

APPENDIX I

For the Record

Year	County Championship	50-Over	4 0-Over National League	t20
2000	5th Div. 1	4th round	6th Div. 1	
2001	2nd Div. 1	winners	4th Div. 1	
2002	8th Div. 1 (R)	runners-up	9th Div. 1 (R)	
2003	7th Div. 2	4th round	9th Div. 2	group
2004	4th Div. 2	3rd round	8th Div. 2	group
2005	8th Div. 2	1st round	6th Div. 2	winners
2006	9th Div. 2	7th group	7th Div. 2	group
2007	1st Div. 2 (P)	6th group	2nd Div. 2 (P)	group
2008	4th Div. 1	quarter-final	6th Div. 1	group
2009	3rd Div. 1	quarter-final	2nd Div. 1	runners-up
2010	2nd Div. 1		runners-up	runners-up
2011	4th Div. 1		runners-up	runners-up
2012	2nd Div. 1		group	semi-finalists

P – promoted   R - relegated

Note: Both the 50-over format and National League 40-over competitions were ditched in 2010 and replaced by one 40-overs per innings tournament. T20 commenced 2003.

First-Class Cricket
Highest Total: 850 for 7 declared v. Middlesex, Taunton 2007
Highest Innings: 342 Justin Langer v. Surrey, Taunton 2006

Limited-Overs Cricket
Highest Total: 50-over 413 for 4 v. Devon, Torquay 1990
                  40-over 377 for 9 v. Sussex, Hove 2003
                  T20   250 for 3 v. Gloucestershire. Taunton 2006

Lowest Total: 50-over 58 v. Middlesex, Southgate 2000
                  40-over 58 v. Essex, Chelmsford 1977
                  T20   82 v. Kent, Taunton 2010

Highest Innings: 50-over 162* C.J. Tavaré v. Devon, Torquay 1990
                  40-over 184 M.E. Trescothick v Gloucestershire, Taunton 2008
                  T20   141* C.L. White v Worcestershire, Worcester 2006

Best Bowling: 50-over 8 for 66 S.R.G. Francis v. Derbyshire, Derby 2004
                  40-over 6 for 24 I.V.A. Richards v. Lancashire, Manchester 1983
                  T20   6 for 5 A.V. Suppiah v. Glamorgan, Cardiff 2011

Chaggi's Celebratory Breakfast

(In honour of Somerset Sabres' victory over
Deccan Chargers, Hyderabad, October 10th, 2009.)

SERVES 2

Ingredients

Veggie oil
A handful of raw cashews
Half teaspoon of mustard seeds
Half teaspoon of cumin seeds
Good sprinkle of tumeric
Four or five curry leaves (optional)
Half a deseeded green chilli, finely chopped
Good sprinkle of chilli powder
Half a red onion, chopped
One or two tomatoes, chopped
White bread
Slosh of water
Handful of chopped coriander leaves
Sprinkle of salt

Method:

Cut up 4 slices of white bread, crusts removed, 6 slices if feeling hungry.
Fry cashews in oil until light brown.
Add mustard seeds and cumin seeds, tumeric, curry leaves, fresh chilli and chilli powder.
Fry spices for a few seconds.
Add onion and tomato and continue frying for a minute or two.
Add bread and mix thoroughly.
Add water and mix to an agreeable consistency – trial and error.
Add coriander leaves and salt. Stir while singing:

'Where be that Blackbird to? I know where he be,
He be up yon Wurzel tree, And I be after he!
Now I sees he, And he sees I,
Buggered if I don't get 'en
With a gurt big stick I'll knock 'im down
Blackbird I'll 'ave he!'

… and serve.